AF225156

TEACHER'S PET PUBLICATIONS

LITPLAN TEACHER PACK
for
The Time Machine
based on the book by
H.G. Wells

Written by
Susan Woodward

© 2008 Teacher's Pet Publications
All Rights Reserved

Copyright Teacher's Pet Publications 2008

Only the student materials in this unit plan (such as worksheets,
study questions, and tests) may be reproduced multiple times
for use in the purchaser's classroom.

For any additional copyright questions,
contact Teacher's Pet Publications.

www.tpet.com

TABLE OF CONTENTS - *The Time Machine*

H.G. Wells

Herbert George Wells was born in Bromley, Kent County, England on September 21, 1866 to Sarah Neal (a domestic servant) and Joseph Wells (a shop owner and professional cricket player). An accident at the age of seven left H. G. bedridden. While his broken leg healed, he discovered the world of books. He enrolled in the Thomas Orley Academy, but his formal education was cut short when his father Joseph broke his thigh, thereby ending his cricket career. Herbert and his older brothers were forced to work as apprentices to help the family's financial situation. His parents separated, and H. G. remained living with his father.

In 1883, Herbert won a scholarship to the Normal School of Science in London, and it was here that he realized his interest in the sciences. This ended up serving him well as an author of science fiction novels such as *The Time Machine* (1895), *The Island of Dr. Moreau* (1896), *The Invisible Man* (1897), and *The War of the Worlds* (1898). Unfortunately, Wells lost his scholarship when he did not fulfill the requirements for the degree, and he was forced to move in with his aunt and uncle in London. He was given a job as a tutor and as a part time faculty member at his uncle's school. It was while he was living with them that he met and eventually married his cousin Isabel Mary in 1891. Four years later, he left Isbel for one of his students, Amy Catherine Robbins. He had two children with Amy Catherine: George Phillip and Frank Richard.

H. G. Wells also had numerous love affairs, two of which produced his daughter Anna Jane (by writer Amber Reeves) and son Anthony West (by author and feminist Rebecca West). Although Amy Catherine knew about most of the affairs, she remained married to H. G. Wells until her death in 1927.

In much of his writing, H. G. Wells sought to create a better way to organize society. This led to the creation of several Utopian novels such as *The Work, Wealth and Happiness of Mankind* (1931) and *The Shape of Things to Come* (1933). His politics leaned toward socialism, and his name was often linked with the socialist parties. Wells was, however, disillusined with socialist leaders Karl Marx and Joseph Stalin because he felt that they were too rigid and restrictive of independent thought.

On August 13, 1946, H. G. Wells died of liver cancer at his London home.

This LitPlan has been designed to develop students' reading, writing, thinking, and lauguage skills through exercises and activities related to *The Time Machine*. It includes sixteen lessons, supported by extra resource materials.

The **introductory lesson** introduces students to the science fiction genre of literature. Following the introductory activity, students are given a transition to explain how the activity relates to the book they are about to read. Following the transition, students are given the materials they will be using during the unit. At the end of the lesson, students begin the pre-reading work for the first reading assignment.

The **reading assignments** are approximately thirty pages each; some are a little shorter while others are a little longer. Students have approximately 15 minutes of pre-reading work to do prior to each reading assignment. This pre-reading work involves reviewing the study questions for the assignment and doing some vocabulary work for selected vocabulary words they will encounter in their reading.

The **study guide questions** are fact-based questions right in the text. These questions come in two formats: short answer or multiple choice. The best use of these materials is probably to use the short answer version of the questions as study guides for students (since answers will be more complete), and to use the multiple choice version for occasional quizzes.

The **vocabulary work** is intended to enrich students' vocabularies as well as to aid in the students' understanding of the book. Prior to each reading assignment, students will complete a two-part worksheet for selected vocabulary words in the upcoming reading assignment. Part I focuses on students' use of general knowledge and contextual clues by giving the sentence in which the word appears in the text. Students are then to write down what they think the words mean based on the words' usage. Part II nails down the definitions of the words by giving students dictionary definitions of the words and having students match the words to the correct definitions based on the words' contextual usage. Students should then have an understanding of the words when they meet them in the text.

After each reading assignment, students will go back and formulate answers for the study guide questions. Discussion of these questions serves as a **review** of the most important events and ideas presented in the reading assignments.

After students complete reading the work, there is a **vocabulary review** lesson which pulls together all of the fragmented vocabulary lists for the reading assignments and gives students a review of all of the words thay have studied.

Following the vocabulary review, a lesson is devoted to the **extra discussion questions/writing assignments**. These questions focus on interpretation, critical analysis, and personal response, employing a variety of thinking skills and adding to the students' understanding of the novel.

There is a **group theme project** in this unit. Student groups will select a science fiction author from a predetermined list. Each group will complete a brief biographical sketch of the author, read two short works (short stories) by the author, and complete a poster. The groups will present their information and explain how the literary works by this author fit the science fiction genre.

There are three **writing assignments** in this unit, each with the purpose of informing, persuading, or expressing personal opinions. The group theme project will count as the informative piece for each student. In Writing Assignment #2, students will write an account of going back in time and changing an event from the past. They will reflect what other events will have been influenced as a result. In the third writing assignment, students will select a quotation from a list and demonstrate how the main idea of the quotation is supported in the novel *The Time Machine*.

There is a **non-fiction reading assignment.** Students must read non-fiction articles, books, etc. to gather information about scientific advances of the nineteenth century. Each student will focus on one advancement in particular and demonstrate how it is reflected in the literature of that time.

The **review lesson** pulls together all of the aspects of the unit. The teacher is given four or five choices of activities or games to use which all serve the same basic function of reviewing all of the information presented in the unit.

The **unit test** comes in two formats: multiple choice or short answer. As a convenience, two different tests for each format have been included. There is also an advanced short answer unit test for advanced students.

There are additional **support materials** included with this unit. The **Unit Resource Materials** section includes suggestions for an in-class library, crossword and word search puzzles related to the novel, and extra worksheets. There is a list of **bulletin board ideas** which gives the teacher suggestions for bulletin boards to go along with this unit. In addition, there is a list of **extra class activities** the teacher could choose from to enhance the unit or as a substitution for an exercise the teacher might feel is inappropriate for his/her class. **Answer keys** are located directly after the **reproducible materials** throughout the unit. The **Vocabulary Resource Materials** section includes similar worksheets and games to reinforce the vocabulary words.

The **level** of this unit can be varied depending upon the criteria on which the individual assignments are graded, the teacher's expectations of his/her students in class discussions, and the formats chosen for the study guides, quizzes and test. If teachers have other ideas/activities they wish to use, they can usually easily be inserted prior to the review lesson.

The student materials may be reproduced for use in the teacher's classroom without infringement of copyrights. No other portion of this unit may be reproduced without the written consent of Teacher's Pet Publications, Inc.

UNIT OBJECTIVES *The Time Machine*

1. Through reading H. G. Wells's *The Time Machine*, students will explore the science fiction genre and its elements.

2. Students will demonstate their understanding of the text on four levels: factual, interpretive, critical, and personal.

3. Students will explore the scientific advancements of the 19th Century and their impact upon fiction writing.

4. Students will be given the opportunity to practice reading orally and silently to improve their skills in each area.

5. Students will answer questions to demonstrate their knowledge and understanding of the main events and characters in *The Time Machine* as they relate to the author's theme development.

6. Students will enrich their vocabularies and improve their understanding of the novel through the vocabulary lessons prepared for use in conjunction with the novel.

7. The writing assignments in this unit are geared to several purposes:
   a. To check the students' reading comprehension
   b. To make students think about the ideas presented by the novel
   c. To encourage logical thinking
   d. To provide an opportunity to practice good grammar and improve students' use of the English language
   e. To have students demonstrate their abilities to inform, to persuade, or to express their own personal ideas

   Note: Students will demonstrate the ability to write effectively to <u>inform</u> by developing and organizing facts to convey information. Students will demonstrate the ability to write effectively to <u>persuade</u> by selecting and organizing relevant information, establishing an argumentative purpose, and by designing an appropriate strategy for an identified audience. Students will demonstrate the ability to write effectively to <u>express personal ideas</u> by selecting a form and its appropriate elements.

8. Students will read aloud, report, and participate in large and small group discussions to improve their public speaking and personal interaction skills.

Date Assigned	Assignment	Completion Date
	Assignment 1 Chapters 1-2	
	Assignment 2 Chapters 3-4	
	Assignment 3 Chapters 5-6	
	Assignment 4 Chapters 7-8	
	Assignment 5 Chapters 9-10	
	Assignment 6 Chapters 11-12 and Epilogue	

1	2	3	4	5
Intro to H. G. Wells and the Science Fiction Genre PVR Ch. 1-2	Study ?s Ch. 1-2 Non-Fiction work: Library/Media Center PVR Ch. 3-4	Study ?s Ch. 3-4 Quiz Ch. 1-4 PVR Ch. 5-6	Study ?s Ch. 5-6 Who Came to Dinner? PVR Ch. 7-8	Study ?s Ch. 7-8 Quiz Ch. 5-8 Group Theme Project (Writing Assignment #1): Library PVR Ch. 9-10
6	7	8	9	10
Study ?s Ch. 9-10 Share Non-Fiction Work PVR Ch. 11-12 and Epilogue	Study ?s Ch. 11-12 and Epilogue Quiz Ch. 9-end Writing Assignment #2 "Blast to the Past"	Group Work: Sci-Fi Authors (creation of poster)	Vocabulary Review	Group Work: Extra Discussion Questions
11	12	13	14	15
In-Class Writing (Assignment #3): Supporting a critical lens	Peer Editing: Assignment #3	Presentations Day 1: Sci-Fi Authors	Presentations Day 2: Sci-Fi Authors	Unit Review
16				
Unit Test				

Key: P = Preview Study Questions   V = Vocabulary Work   R = Read

STUDY GUIDE QUESTIONS

Assignment 1
Chapters 1-2

1. According to the Time Traveller, what four extensions must any real body have in order to exist?
2. What does the Time Traveller say is the fourth dimension?
3. How does the Time Traveller intend to prove his theory of time travel?
4. What do the men see when the Psychologist presses the lever on the Time Machine model?
5. What does the Time Traveller show his guests after they witness his experiment?
6. The Time Traveller is late for the second dinner party. What is in the note he left for the Medical Man?
7. What is the condition of the Time Traveller when he enters the dining room?
8. When the Time Traveller leaves the dining room to wash and dress, what does the narrator notice about him?
9. The narrator considers following the Time Traveller from the room but doesn't. Why not?
10. Who seems to become the most nervous when the Time Traveller sits down to dinner?

Assignment 2
Chapters 3-4

1. What prohibits the Time Traveller from using his machine as he had planned?
2. What does the Time Traveller notice when he tests the machine for the very first time?
3. What does the Time Traveller fear will happen if he stops the machine?
4. What does the Time Traveller see when he stops the machine in the garden?
5. What does the Time Traveller do when the little people attempt to explore the machine?
6. Into what year does the Time Traveller estimate he has arrived?
7. How does the Time Traveller describe the little people who come to greet him?
8. Where does the Time Traveller think the inhabitants of the land believe he came from?
9. How does the Time Traveller describe the land of the little people?
10. What does the Time Traveller notice about the little people and their society?

Assignment 3
Chapters 5-6

1. What does the Time Traveller discover when he returns to the area surrounding the White Sphinx on the first night?
2. Although he is in great distress over the missing Time Machine, what one fact makes the Time Traveller feel assured?
3. When the Time Traveller goes to the second great hall trying to find the Time Machine, what does he use that the little people have forgotten?
4. What clues does the Time Traveller find that lead him to believe he knows the whereabouts of the time machine?

5. What reaction does the Time Traveller receive when he suggests opening the doors to the bronze pedestal?

6. How do the Time Traveller and Weena become friends?

7. How does the Time Traveller describe the strange creature he encounters in a colossal ruin near the great hall?

8. To what conclusion does the Time Traveller come regarding the creature he watched vanish down a deep shaft?

9. Why does the Time Traveller postpone going underground to find the time machine?

10. What does the Time Traveller learn about the diet of the Morlocks?

Assignment 4
Chapters 7-8

1. Why does the Time Traveller regard the new moon as his enemy?

2. What souvenir from the future world does the Time Traveller remove from his pocket to show his dinner guests?

3. What kind of meat does the Time Traveller believe he saw on the table in the Morlocks' cavern?

4. What confuses the Time Traveller about the stars?

5. Why does the Time Traveller throw his shoes away?

6. What weapon does the Time Traveller believe would be the most effective against the Morlocks?

7. What is the Palace of Green Porcelain?

8. After finding a block of sulphur in one of the galleries, what does the Time Traveller think about making? Does he make it?

9. Why does the Time Traveller break a lever off one of the machines he discovers?

10. What does the Time Traveller find in one of the museum galleries that literally makes him dance?

Assignment 5
Chapters 9-10

1. What does the Time Traveller do that he later discovers to be an "atrocious folly?"

2. What is the result of the Time Traveller's maneuvering with the matches and helping Weena when they are accosted by the Morlocks in the woods?

3. What do the Morlocks take from the Time Traveller's pocket?

4. What is the source of the "slumberous murmur" the Time Traveller hears in the forest?

5. What discovery does the Time Traveller make as he "walked over the smoking ashes under the bright sky?"

6. What does the Time Traveller see when he finally approaches the pedestal of the sphinx?"

7. What does the Time Traveller notice about the Time Machine when he finds it?

8. What happens when the Time Traveller enters the pedestal to inspect the machine?

9. The Time Traveller prepares to put the levers back into the machine, what "one little thing" does he realize he has overlooked?

10. How does the Time Traveller finally escape the Morlocks?

Assignment 6

<u>Chapters 11-12 and Epilogue</u>

1. What does the Time Traveller notice when he looks at the dials of the Time Machine after escaping the Morlocks?

2. When the Time Traveller stops again, after escaping the Morlocks, what is the earth like?

3. The Time Traveller stops on a beach. What type of creatures surround the Time Machine?

4. After escaping from the crab creatures, the Time Traveller goes thirty million years into the future. What does he see?

5. When the Time Traveller returns home, why does the Time Machine land in the a different place than it had left?

6. What does the Time Traveller find that confirms he has arrived back in time on the correct date?

7. Who is the first to speak after the Time Traveller completes his fantastic tale?

8. What does the Medical Man find to be "a curious thing?"

9. What becomes of the Time Traveller?

10. What does the Narrator have as a reminder "that even when mind and strength had gone, gratitude and a mutual tenderness still lived in the heart of Man?"

Assignment 1
Chapters 1-2

1. According to the Time Traveller, what four extensions must any real body have in order to exist?
The Time Traveller claims that any real body must have length, breadth, thickness, and duration in order to exist.

2. What does the Time Traveller say is the fourth dimension?
The Time Traveller says that time is the fourth dimension.

3. How does the Time Traveller intend to prove his theory of time travel?
The Time Traveller intends to prove his theory with the use of a small model of his Time Machine.

4. What do the men see when the Psychologist presses the lever on the Time Machine model?
When the Psychologist presses the lever on the Time Machine model, the machine disappears and no one knows where it is.

5. What does the Time Traveller show his guests after they witness his experiment?
He shows the group a life-sized Time Machine intended for his use.

6. The Time Traveller is late for the second dinner party. What is in the note he left for the Medical Man?
The note instructs the group to start dinner promptly at seven o'clock if he isn't there. It also says he will join them as soon as he can.

7. What is the condition of the Time Traveller when he enters the dining room?
His coat is dusty, dirty, and smeared with green down the sleeves; his hair is disordered and greyer; his face is ghastly pale, and there is a half-healed cut on his chin.

8. When the Time Traveller leaves the dining room to wash and dress, what does the narrator notice about him?
The Time Traveller is not wearing shoes, and his feet and socks are bloody.

9. The narrator considers following the Time Traveller from the room but doesn't. Why not?
He remembers how much the Time Traveller detests any fuss about him.

10. Who seems to become the most nervous when the Time Traveller sits down to dinner?
The Silent Man seems to be the most nervous.

Assignment 2
Chapters 3-4

1. What prohibits the Time Traveller from using his machine as he had planned?
One of the nickel bars for the machine is too short and has to be fixed before the machine can be used.

2. What does the Time Traveller notice when he tests the machine for the very first time?
He notices the clock in his laboratory goes from 10:01 to 3:20 in a matter of seconds.

3. What does the Time Traveller fear will happen if he stops the machine?
He fears that if he stops the machine, he might blow up into the unknown.

4. What does the Time Traveller see when he stops the machine in the garden?
He sees a lawn surrounded by rhododendron bushes and a colossal white marble figure in the shape of a winged sphinx.

5. What does the Time Traveller do when the little people attempt to explore the machine?
To prevent them from accidentally setting the machine in motion, he unscrews the levers and puts them in his pocket.

6. Into what year does the Time Traveller estimate he has arrived?
The Time Traveller estimates that he has arrived in the year 802,701 A.D.

7. How does the Time Traveller describe the little people who come to greet him?
The little people have curly hair, but none on the face or neck; they have small ears, small mouths with bright, thin lips, pointed chins, and mild eyes.

8. Where does the Time Traveller think the inhabitants of the land believe he came from?
He is certain the little people think he came from the sun in a thunderstorm.

9. How does the Time Traveller describe the land of the little people?
The land is filled with green plants and trees. There are ruined buildings in the distance. He notices the huge amount of flowers and fruit trees everywhere. He feels there is nothing ugly in this place.

10. What does the Time Traveller notice about the little people and their society?
He notices that no one seems to do work of any kind, and they do not live in separate houses, but in sort of communal buildings. He also notes they eat only fruits and absolutely no meat. He feels as if he is in some kind of utopia.

Assignment 3
<u>Chapters 5-6</u>

1. What does the Time Traveller discover when he returns to the area surrounding the White Sphinx on the first night?
He discovers the Time Machine is gone.

2. Although he is in great distress over the missing Time Machine, what one fact makes the Time Traveller feel assured?
The Time Machine could not have been moved in time because he has the levers in his pocket. It has to have been moved to a different location in the present time.

3. When the Time Traveller goes to the second great hall trying to find the Time Machine, what does he use that the little people have forgotten?
He uses matches.

4. What clues does the Time Traveller find that lead him to believe he knows the whereabouts of the time machine?
He finds a groove and a series of footprints on the ground leading to the bronze pedestal of the statue.

5. What reaction does the Time Traveller receive when he suggests opening the doors to the bronze pedestal?
The little people become visibly upset.

6. How do the Time Traveller and Weena become friends?
The Time Traveller saves her from drowning in the river.

7. How does the Time Traveller describe the strange creature he encounters in a colossal ruin near the great hall?
The creature is a dull white, ape-like creature with large grayish-red eyes. It has flaxen hair on its head and down its back.

8. To what conclusion does the Time Traveller come regarding the creature he watched vanish down a deep shaft?
He believes there must be an underground society living in a great tunnel system beneath the world above.

9.   Why does the Time Traveller postpone going underground to find the time machine?
He is afraid because he is alone.

10.   What does the Time Traveller learn about the diet of the Morlocks?
He learns the Morlocks are meat eaters.

Assignment 4
Chapters 7-8

1.   Why does the Time Traveller regard the new moon as his enemy?
He dreads the darkness of the new moon because the Morlocks come out in the dark.

2.   What souvenir from the future world does the Time Traveller remove from his pocket to show his dinner guests?
He removes two wilted flowers that Weena had given to him.

3.   What kind of meat does the Time Traveller believe he saw on the table in the Morlocks' cavern?
The Time Traveller is certain that the pieces of meat he'd seen on the table were captured Eloi (upper world people).

4.   What confuses the Time Traveller about the stars?
The constellations he knows are gone because the stars have repositioned themselves over time.

5.   Why does the Time Traveller throw his shoes away?
A nail from the heel of the shoe is pressing into his foot, and it causes his ankle to swell terribly.

6.   What weapon does the Time Traveller believe would be the most effective against the Morlocks?
He believes fire would be the best weapon against the Morlocks.

7.   What is the Palace of Green Porcelain?
The Palace of Green Porcelain is a museum.

8.   After finding a block of sulphur in one of the galleries, what does the Time Traveller think about making? Does he make it?
He wonders if he could find the proper ingredients to make gunpowder. There is no saltpeter to be found, so he cannot make any gunpowder.

9.   Why does the Time Traveller break a lever off one of the machines he discovers?
He breaks the lever off to use as a mace against the Morlocks.

10.   What does the Time Traveller find in one of the museum galleries that literally makes him dance?
He finds a box of matches that are still good.

Assignment 5
Chapters 9-10

1.   What does the Time Traveller do that he later discovers to be an "atrocious folly?"
He lights the firewood to cover his retreat from the Morlocks.

2.   What is the result of the Time Traveller's maneuvering with the matches and helping Weena when they are accosted by the Morlocks in the woods?
He realizes he is turned around within the woods so badly he has lost his sense of direction.

3.   What do the Morlocks take from the Time Traveller's pocket?
They take his box of matches while he sleeps.

4. What is the source of the "slumberous murmur" the Time Traveller hears in the forest?
   The fire the Time Traveller set earlier to scare the Morlocks has become a raging inferno burning the entire forest.

5. What discovery does the Time Traveller make as he "walked over the smoking ashes under the bright sky?"
   He discovers he still has a few loose matches in his pocket that must have fallen out of the box.

6. What does the Time Traveller see when he finally approaches the pedestal of the sphinx?
   He discovers the bronze doors to the pedestal are open.

7. What does the Time Traveller notice about the Time Machine when he finds it?
   He discovers that the Morlocks have oiled and cleaned the machine thoroughly.

8. What happens when the Time Traveller enters the pedestal to inspect the machine?
   The doors to the pedestal snap shut, trapping him inside with the Morlocks.

9. As the Time Traveller prepares to put the levers back into the machine, what "one little thing" does he realize he has overlooked?
   He tries to light the matches to scare the Morlocks, but realizes he cannot light them without the match box.

10. How does the Time Traveller finally escape the Morlocks?
    He fights the Morlocks while he inserts the levers. He is finally able to operate the Time Machine and disappear.

Assignment 6
Chapters 11-12 and Epilogue

1. What does the Time Traveller notice when he looks at the dials of the Time Machine after escaping the Morlocks?
   He notices he is traveling further into the future.

2. When the Time Traveller stops again, after escaping the Morlocks, what is the earth like?
   It's a very dark, dismal place because the earth no longer turns on its axis. The Time Traveller has landed on the dark side of the planet.

3. The Time Traveller stops on a beach. What type of creatures surround the Time Machine?
   The machine is surrounded by giant crab-like creatures with long antennae, many legs, and smeared with slime.

4. After escaping from the crab creatures, the Time Traveller goes thirty million years into the future. What does he see?
   The world is even darker than the world he just left. It is cold and snowy and absolutely silent. He sees no recognizable signs of life except for liverworts and lichen, and a football-sized creature with tentacles.

5. When the Time Traveller returns home, why does the Time Machine land in a different place than it had left?
   When the Time Traveller landed in the world of Eloi, the Morlocks had dragged the machine inside the pedestal. That accounts for the machine returning to the laboratory in a different location.

6. What does the Time Traveller find that confirms he has arrived back in time on the correct date?
   He finds a copy of the Pall Mall Gazette on the table by the door, which confirms the date he arrived home.

7. Who is the first to speak after the Time Traveller completes his fantastic tale?
   The Editor comments first by saying that it is a pity the Time Traveller is not a writer of stories.

8. What does the Medical Man find to be "a curious thing?"
   The Medical Man finds it curious that he does not know the natural order of the two flowers the Time Traveller produces from his pocket.

9. What becomes of the Time Traveller?
   The Narrator sees him in the Time Machine, and then he vanishes. The Time Traveller never returns.

10. What does the Narrator have as a reminder "that even when mind and strength had gone, gratitude and a mutual tenderness still lived in the heart of Man?"
    The Narrator keeps the two wilted flowers Weena had given the Time Traveller.

Assignment 1
Chapters 1-2

1. According to the Time Traveller, what four extensions must any real body have in order to exist?
   A. Height, width, volume, and velocity
   B. Length, breadth, thickness, and weight
   C. Light, sound, weight, and opaqueness
   D. Length, breadth, thickness, and duration

2. What does the Time Traveller say is the fourth dimension?
   A. Width
   B. Volume
   C. Time
   D. Length

3. How does the Time Traveller intend to prove his theory of time travel?
   A. He intends to bring items from the past into the present.
   B. He is going to synchronize his watch with the gentlemen's watches and then travel ten minutes into the future.
   C. He plans to send the Psychologist ten minutes into the future.
   D. He has created a small model of his Time Machine to show the men how it works.

4. What do the men see when the Psychologist presses the lever on the Time Machine model?
   A. The Psychologist disappears before their eyes.
   B. The model disappears before their eyes.
   C. The Time Machine explodes in a cloud of smoke.
   D. Nothing happens.

5. What does the Time Traveller show his guests after they witness his experiment?
   A. The Psychologist's watch is one minute behind his own watch.
   B. He shows them his watch, which is precisely ten minutes behind the time on their own watches.
   C. He shows them a life-sized Time Machine he built for his own use.
   D. He shows them the plans for a life-sized model of the Time Machine.

6. The Time Traveller is late for the second dinner party. What is in the note he left for the Medical Man?

   A. The Time Traveller instructs the Medical Man to meet him at his laboratory at precisely 6:48 P.M.

   B. The Time Traveller instructs the Medical Man to contact the police if he is more than one hour late for dinner.

   C. The Time Traveller instructs the Medical Man to begin dinner promptly at 7:00.

   D. The Time Traveller instructs the Medical Man to use the time machine to join him in the future.

7. What is the condition of the Time Traveller when he enters the dining room?

   A. He is dressed for dinner but looks very tired and has lost weight.

   B. His hair is greyer, and he has a half-healed cut on his face. His clothes are dusty and dirty.

   C. He is dressed in a smoking jacket, is carrying a pipe, and is smoking triumphantly.

   D. He is feverish, collapses into the room, and becomes unconscious.

8. When the Time Traveller leaves the dining room to wash and dress, what does the narrator notice about him?

   A. He notices the Time Traveller has developed a nervous tick.

   B. He notices the Time Traveller's hair has become stark white.

   C. He notices the Time Traveller's clothes look two sizes too large.

   D. He notices the Time Traveller is not wearing shoes, and his feet and socks are bloody.

9. The narrator considers following the Time Traveller from the room but doesn't. Why not?

   A. He is irritated with the Time Traveller's attitude and refuses to follow him.

   B. He remembers how much the Time Traveller detests any fuss about him.

   C. He wants to speak to the Medical Man about the Time Traveller.

   D. He decides the Time Traveller needs privacy to wash and dress for dinner.

10. Who seems to become the most nervous when the Time Traveller sits down to dinner?

   A. The Psychologist

   B. The Narrator

   C. The Silent Man

   D. The Medical Man

1. What prohibits the Time Traveller from using his machine as he had planned?

   A. He is suffering from a terrible fever that has lasted for five days.

   B. He is afraid to use the machine because he doesn't know if he will survive the trip.

   C. One of the nickel bars is too short and has to be replaced.

   D. He discovers the machine does not work, and he has to rebuild it.

2. What does the Time Traveller notice when he uses the machine for the very first time?

   A. The crystal needed to activate the machine is cracked.

   B. The time on the clock goes from 10:01 to 3:30.

   C. He feels like he is sleep walking.

   D. Nothing happens when he tries the machine the first time.

3. What does the Time Traveller fear will happen if he stops the machine?

   A. He is afraid he will not be able to find the fuel needed to run the machine.

   B. He is afraid the machine will not stop at all.

   C. He is afraid he will never return to his own time period.

   D. He is afraid he will blow up into the unknown.

4. What does the Time Traveller see when he stops the machine in the garden?

   A. He sees a lawn surrounded by rhododendron bushes and a colossal white marble figure in the shape of a winged sphinx.

   B. He sees the moon and realizes it is too close to the earth.

   C. He sees a small village in the distance, but no people.

   D. He sees a huge castle made of glass.

5. What does the Time Traveller do when the little people attempt to explore the machine?

   A. He gets back in the machine and leaves.

   B. He distracts their attention by walking away from the machine.

   C. He yells and waves them away from the machine.

   D. He unscrews the levers that make the machine work and puts them in his pocket.

6. Into what year does the Time Traveller estimate he has arrived?

   A. 2051 AD

   B. 802,701 AD

   C. 874,286 BC

   D. 1066 AD

7.   How does the Time Traveller describe the little people who come to greet him?
   A. They are pale-complexioned with flaxen hair and greyish-red eyes.
   B. They are extremely tall and bronze with superhuman strength.
   C. They are small with long, straight hair, pale lips, and wild eyes.
   D. They are small with curly hair, bright lips, pointed chins, and mild eyes.

8.   Where does the Time Traveller think the inhabitants of the land believe he came from?
   A. They believe he came from the other side of the planet.
   B. They believe he came from the moon.
   C. They believe he came from below ground.
   D. They believe he came from the sun during a thunderstorm.

9.   Which best describes the land of the little people?
   A. It is a vast wasteland.
   B. The land is filled with green plants and trees, huge amounts of flowers, and there are ruins in the distance.
   C. It is a huge desert with a mountain range in the far distance.
   D. The natural landscape is masked by huge glass buildings and extensive roads.

10.   What does the Time Traveller notice about the little people and their society?
   A. The people have superhuman intelligence and are able to move things with their minds.
   B. Both the men and the women are fierce hunters and warriors.
   C. They are a contemplative society that spends days discussing philosophical issues.
   D. No one seems to do any work. They eat fruit all day and sleep in communal houses.

1. What does the Time Traveller discover when he returns to the area surrounding the White Sphinx on the first night?

   A. The statue of the White Sphinx has been beheaded.

   B. He discovers the Time Machine is gone.

   C. He finds a young boy examining the Time Machine closely.

   D. Someone has smashed the dials of the Time Machine.

2. Although he is in great distress over the missing Time Machine, what one fact makes the Time Traveller feel reassured?

   A. He knew even if he could not get home, he would be very happy living with the little people.

   B. He has the plans to the machine in his pocket and can build a new machine.

   C. He has the key to start the machine in his pocket.

   D. He has the levers to work the machine in his pocket.

3. When the Time Traveller goes to the second great hall trying to find the Time Machine, what item does he use that the little people have forgotten?

   A. Matches

   B. Eye glasses

   C. Magnifying glasses

   D. Scissors

4. What clue does the Time Traveller find that leads him to believe he knows the whereabouts of the Time Machine?

   A. There is a trail of broken parts leading into the forest.

   B. There is a note in his pocket telling him the machine has been "borrowed."

   C. There are grooves and footprints in the dirt in front of the bronze pedestal.

   D. He overhears a group of the people talking; they mention a cave in the forest.

5. What reaction does the Time Traveller receive when he suggests opening the doors to the bronze pedestal?

   A. The little people begin banging on the doors.

   B. The little people become very happy.

   C. The little people become visibly upset.

   D. The little people ignore him and go about their business.

6.   How do the Time Traveller and Weena become friends?
      A.   The Time Traveller saves her from drowning.
      B.   Weena's father gives her to the Time Traveller as a gift.
      C.   He asks her to serve as a guide into the wilderness as he looks for his Time
           Machine.
      D.   Weena feels pity for him because he is alone, so she hangs out with him.

7.   How does the Time Traveller describe the strange creature he encounters in a colossal
      ruin near the great hall?
      A.   He sees a great serpent with bright yellow eyes and huge fangs.
      B.   He sees a huge spider-like creature with large claws, long antennae, and many
           legs.
      C.   He sees a dull white, ape-like creature with grayish-red eyes.
      D.   He sees a seven-foot man-like creature covered with fur.

8.   To what conclusion does the Time Traveller come regarding the creature he watched
      vanish down a deep shaft?
      A.   He realizes that spiders have evolved and now live underground.
      B.   The giant creature is strong enough to carry the Time Machine away.
      C.   The creature must belong to some underground society that lives in tunnels below.
      D.   The serpent is what caused the little people so much fear.

9.   Why does the Time Traveller postpone going underground to find the Time Machine?
      A.   He is terrified of the dark.
      B.   He is afraid he will not be able to find his way back.
      C.   He is afraid because he is alone.
      D.   He has been sick and is waiting to regain his strength.

10.   What does the Time Traveller learn about the diet of the Morlocks?
      A.   They are vegetarians.
      B.   They eat the rodents that live in their caves.
      C.   They are carnivores.
      D.   They only eat once a week.

Assignment 4
Chapters 7-8

1. Why does the Time Traveller regard the new moon as his enemy?
    A. With every passing of the new moon the Time Traveller fears he will never return home again.
    B. He dreads the darkness of the new moon because he is running out of matches.
    C. He dreads the darkness of the new moon because the Morlocks come out in the dark.
    D. With every passing of the new moon an Eloi must be given to the Morlocks.

2. What souvenir from the future world does the Time Traveller remove from his pocket to show his dinner guests?
    A. A lump of camphor
    B. A necklace made by Weena
    C. A box of matches
    D. Two wilted flowers

3. What is the "clear knowledge" regarding the meat seen by the Time Traveller in the Morlocks' caverns?
    A. The meat on the white table is an Eloi; the Morlocks eat them.
    B. The Morlocks use the meat to try to capture the giant serpent that lives underground.
    C. The meat is placed there as bait to draw the Time Traveller into the caverns.
    D. The Morlocks are cannibals; they eat each other.

4. What confuses the Time Traveller about the stars?
    A. He tries to find the North Star but can not determine which one it is.
    B. There are no stars in the sky.
    C. The familiar constellations are no longer in the sky.
    D. They are so close to the earth that they reflect light, even at nighttime.

5. Why does the Time Traveller throw his shoes away?
    A. A nail keeps poking him in the heel, and his ankle has become swollen.
    B. The shoes leave specific footprints for the Morlocks to follow.
    C. He tries to blend in with the Eloi, so he discards all his clothing from his own time.
    D. He no longer needs them.

6.   What weapon does the Time Traveller believe would be the most effective against the
       Morlocks?
       A. Fire
       B. Dynamite
       C. A mace
       D. A crossbow

7.   What is the Palace of Green Porcelain?
       A. It is the Time Traveller's own house.
       B. It is an ancient bank.
       C. It is an ancient museum.
       D. It is an ancient train station.

8.   After finding a block of sulphur in one of the galleries, what idea sets the Time
       Traveller's mind racing?
       A. He can use all the blocks he's found to create a stronghold for himself.
       B. He can place the lighted sulphur blocks at the openings of the Morlocks' caves to
           keep them in at night.
       C. He wonders if he can find the proper ingredients to make gunpowder.
       D. He believes the terrible smell of sulphur burning will keep the Morlocks away.

9.   Why does the Time Traveller break a lever off one of the machines he discovers?
       A. He uses it to brace the doors to the museum closed.
       B. He uses the lever as a weapon against the Morlocks.
       C. He intentionally breaks the machine so the Morlocks can't use it.
       D. He is trying to make a new lever so the Time Machine will work.

10.   What does the Time Traveller find in one of the galleries that literally makes him dance?
       A. He finds a box of matches.
       B. He finds books that he himself had published about time travel.
       C. He finds canned foods that are still good enough to eat.
       D. He finds two workable sticks of dynamite.

Assignment 5
Chapters 9-10

1.   What does the Time Traveller do that he later discovers to be an "atrocious folly?"
     A.   He lights the firewood to frighten the Morlocks.
     B.   He leaves Weena unguarded near a hollow tree.
     C.   He runs into the woods without first checking his whereabouts.
     D.   He throws the sticks of dynamite at the Morlocks.

2.   What is the result of the Time Traveller's maneuvering with the matches and helping Weena when they are accosted by the Morlocks in the woods?
     A.   He falls against a tree and is knocked unconscious.
     B.   He loses his sense of direction and does not know which way to go to safety.
     C.   The Morlocks attack, and the Time Traveller breaks his arm fighting them.
     D.   The Morlocks kill Weena.

3.   What do the Morlocks take from the Time Traveller's pocket?
     A.   They take the two flowers that Weena had given him.
     B.   They take his compass.
     C.   They take the two sticks of dynamite.
     D.   They take the box of matches.

4.   What is the source of the "slumberous murmur" the Time Traveller hears in the forest?
     A.   It is the sound the Eloi make trying to scare the Morlocks.
     B.   It is the sound of a forest fire roaring.
     C.   It is the sound of the only creature the Morlocks fear.
     D.   It is the sound of the Time Traveller snoring.

5.   What discovery does the Time Traveller make as he "walked over the smoking ashes under the bright sky?"
     A.   He discovers he still has a few loose matches in his pocket.
     B.   He discovers Weena hiding safely in a large hole.
     C.   He discovers Weena's burned body.
     D.   He discovers the entrance to the cave where his Time Machine is hidden.

6.   What does the Time Traveller see when he finally approaches the pedestal of the sphinx?
     A.   The Eloi have boarded up the entrance to the pedestal.
     B.   The broken stone head of the sphinx is actually the key to get inside the pedestal.
     C.   The doors of the pedestal are standing open.
     D.   The time machine is standing outside the pedestal.

7.   What does the Time Traveller notice about the Time Machine when he finds it?
    A.   The crystal that makes it work is now cracked.
    B.   The Morlocks have cleaned and oiled it thoroughly.
    C.   The dials are broken; he doesn't know if the machine will work.
    D.   It is covered with a slimy film from being underground.

8.   What happens when the Time Traveller enters the pedestal to inspect the machine?
    A.   The doors suddenly close, trapping him inside with the Morlocks.
    B.   A Morlock takes the levers from the Time Traveller and tries to work the machine.
    C.   He is grabbed by Morlocks and tied up.
    D.   The machine starts.

9.   The Time Traveller prepares to put the levers back into the machine, what "one little thing" does he realize he has overlooked?
    A.   He can't start the machine until it is back in the exact spot where he arrived.
    B.   He can't light the matches without the match box.
    C.   He has not fixed the broken lever.
    D.   He has left the matches outside.

10.   How does the Time Traveller finally escape the Morlocks?
    A.   The Eloi come to his rescue and distract the Morlocks long enough for him to leave.
    B.   He throws a stick of dynamite at them and blows them up.
    C.   He lures them to a tunnel he has filled with gunpowder. He then sets off the charge, sealing the Morlocks inside.
    D.   He fights the Morlocks while he inserts the levers into the machine. He is able to turn it on and escape.

Assignment 6
Chapters 11-12 and Epilogue

1. What does the Time Traveller notice when he looks at the dials of the Time Machine after escaping the Morlocks?

    A. He realizes he forgot to set the dials for his own time period.

    B. He notices he is traveling further into the future.

    C. The dials no longer work so he has no idea where he is going.

    D. He notices he is traveling back to prehistoric times.

2. When the Time Traveller stops again after escaping the Morlocks, what is the earth like?

    A. It is covered in water.

    B. It is more beautiful than the Time Traveller remembered.

    C. It is a very dark, dismal place.

    D. It is cold and very dark.

3. The Time Traveller stops on a beach. What type of creatures surround the Time Machine?

    A. They are small, football shaped creatures with slimy tentacles.

    B. They are primitive humans in animal skins who do not possess language skills.

    C. They are super-humans who are able to read the Time Traveller's mind.

    D. They are large crab-like creatures with claws, long antennae, and many legs.

4. After escaping from the crab creatures the Time Traveller goes thirty million years into the future. What does he see?

    A. The world is a dark, mountainous region ruled by primitive humans.

    B. The world is a lush garden paradise.

    C. The world is cold, snowy, and absolutely silent.

    D. It is merely an empty space; the earth has been destroyed.

5. When the Time Traveller returns home, why does the Time Machine land in a different place than it had left?

    A. The machine skids to a stop when the Time Traveller lands.

    B. The orbit of the Earth has changed.

    C. The velocity of passing time has propelled the machine physically forward.

    D. It lands in a different spot because it had been moved by the Morlocks.

6. What does the time Traveller find that confirms he has arrived back in time on the correct date?

    A. He looks at the calendar in his laboratory.
    B. He finds a copy of the *London Times* sitting on his desk; it has the date on it.
    C. He finds a copy of the *Pall Mall Gazette* with the date on it.
    D. His watch keeps track of the date.

7. What does the Editor say after the Time Traveller completes his fantastic tale?

    A. He says the Time Traveller is crazy and insists on calling the authorities.
    B. He says the story must be kept secret from the citizens of the world.
    C. He says he wants to start a committee to study the benefits of time travel.
    D. He says it's a pity the Time Traveller isn't a writer of stories.

8. What does the Medical Man find to be "a curious thing?"

    A. The Time Traveller is covered with nearly-healed wounds as if he'd been injured many days prior.
    B. The Time Traveller seems to believe he has actually traveled through time; the Medical Man thinks he is mad.
    C. He does not recognize the type of flowers the Time Traveller brought back.
    D. The Time Traveller's hair has turned pure white since the Medical Man had seen him one week earlier.

9. What becomes of the Time Traveller?

    A. He becomes world-famous for his invention.
    B. He is committed to an insane asylum.
    C. He is so traumatized by his experiences that he destroys the time machine.
    D. He enters the time machine once more and is never seen again.

10. What does the Narrator have as a reminder "that even when mind and strength had gone, gratitude and a mutual tenderness still lived in the heart of Man?"

    A. The Narrator has the two wilted flowers.
    B. The Narrator has the miniature model of the time machine.
    C. The Narrator has the Time Traveller's journal of his adventures.
    D. The Narrator has become closer friends with the Time Traveller.

ANSWER KEY: STUDY QUESTIONS *The Time Machine*

	1	2	3	4	5	6
1	D	C	B	C	A	B
2	C	B	D	D	B	C
3	D	D	A	A	D	D
4	B	A	C	C	B	C
5	C	D	C	A	A	D
6	C	B	A	A	C	C
7	B	D	C	C	B	D
8	D	D	C	C	A	C
9	B	B	C	B	B	D
10	C	D	C	A	D	A

VOCABULARY WORKSHEETS

Part I: Using Prior Knowledge and Contextual Clues
    Below are the sentences in which the vocabulary words appear in the text. Read the sentence. Use any clues you can find in the sentence combined with your prior knowledge, and write what you think the underlined words mean on the lines provided.

1.   The Time Traveller (for so it will be convenient to speak of him) was expounding a <u>recondite</u> matter to us.

2.   "Our mental existences, which are immaterial and have no dimensions, are passing along the Time-Dimension with a uniform <u>velocity</u> from the cradle to the grave."

3.   "Don't you think it would attract attention?" said the Medical Man. "Our ancestors had no great tolerance for <u>anachronisms</u>."

4.   "Serious objections," remarked the Provincial Mayor, with an air of <u>impartiality</u>, turning towards the Time Traveller.

5.   I remember vividly the flickering light, his queer, broad head in silhouette, the dance of the shadows, how we all followed him, puzzled but <u>incredulous</u>, and how there in the laboratory we beheld a larger edition of the little mechanism which we had seen vanish from before our eyes.

6.   But the Time Traveller had more than a touch of <u>whim</u> among his elements, and we distrusted him.

7.   There was some speculation at the dinner table about the Time Traveller's absence, and I suggested time traveling, in a half-<u>jocular</u> spirit.

8.   "I'm going to wash and dress, and then I'll come down and explain things.... Save me some of that <u>mutton</u>. I'm starved for a bit of meat."

9.   "I want something to eat. I won't say a word until I get some <u>peptone</u> into my arteries."

10.   The Journalist tried to relieve the tension by telling <u>anecdotes</u> of Hettie Potter.

Part II: Determining the Meaning -- Match the vocabulary words to their dictionary definitions.

_____ 1.   RECONDITE   A. Characterized by joking

_____ 2.   VELOCITY   B. Rapidity of motion or operation; swiftness; speed

_____ 3.   ANACHRONISMS   C. Indicating or showing unbelief; skeptical

_____ 4.   IMPARTIALITY   D. Odd or capricious notion or desire; a sudden or freakish fancy

_____ 5.   INCREDULOUS   E. The meat of sheep

_____ 6.   WHIM   F. Dealing with very profound or difficult subject matter

_____ 7.   JOCULAR   G. Complex water-soluble nutrient obtained by digesting protein

_____ 8.   MUTTON   H. Showing no bias; neutrality

_____ 9.   PEPTONE   I. Short accounts of interesting or humorous incidents

_____ 10. ANECDOTES   J. Persons, objects, or practices that belong to a different time period

Part I: Using Prior Knowledge and Contextual Clues
   Below are the sentences in which the vocabulary words appear in the text. Read the sentence. Use any clues you can find in the sentence combined with your prior knowledge, and write what you think the underlined words mean on the lines provided.

1. An <u>eddying</u> murmur filled my ears, and a strange, dumb confusedness descended on my mind.

____

2. "The unpleasant sensations of the start were less <u>poignant</u> now. They merged at last into a kind of hysterical exhilaration."

____

3. "So long as I travelled at a high velocity through time, this scarcely mattered; I was, so to speak, <u>attenuated</u>--was slipping like a vapor through the interstices of intervening substances!"

____

4. "A <u>colossal</u> figure, carved apparently in some white stone, loomed indistinctly beyond the rhododendrons through the hazy downpour."

____

5. "I looked up again at the crouching white shape, and the full <u>temerity</u> of my voyage came suddenly upon me."

____

6. "And perhaps the thing that struck me most was its <u>dilapidated</u> look. The stained-glass windows, which displayed only a geometrical pattern, were broken in many places, and the curtains that hung across the lower end were thick with dust."

____

7. "These people of the remote future were strict vegetarians, and while I was with them, in spite of some carnal cravings, I had to be <u>frugivorous</u> also."

____

8. "But it was slow work, and the little people soon tired and wanted to get away from my interrogations.... I never met people more <u>indolent</u> or more easily fatigued."

____

9. "And the children seemed to my eyes to be but the miniatures of their parents. I judged, then, that the children of that time were extremely <u>precocious</u>, physically at least, and I found afterwards abundant verification of my opinion."

____

10. "The work of <u>ameliorating</u> the conditions of life--the true civilising process that makes life more and more secure--had gone steadily on to a climax."

____

The Time Machine Vocabulary Worksheet Assignment 2 Continued

Part II: Determining the Meaning -- Match the vocabulary words to their dictionary definitions.

_____ 1.	EDDYING	A.	Extraordinarily great in size, extent, or degree; gigantic; huge
_____ 2.	POIGNANT	B.	Affecting or moving the emotions
_____ 3.	ATTENUATED	C.	Reckless boldness; rashness
_____ 4.	COLOSSAL	D.	Feeding on fruit; fruit eating
_____ 5.	TEMERITY	E.	To make thin; to make slender or fine
_____ 6.	DILAPIDATED	F.	Unusually advanced or mature in development, esp. mentally
_____ 7.	FRUGIVOROUS	G.	Fallen into partial ruin or decay, as from age, wear, or neglect
_____ 8.	INDOLENT	H.	Showing a disposition to avoid exertion; slothful; lazy
_____ 9.	PRECOCIOUS	I.	Swirling as if in a whirlpool
_____ 10.	AMELIORATING	J.	Making better, more bearable, or more satisfactory; improving

VOCABULARY ASSIGNMENT 3 *The Time Machine*

Part I: Using Prior Knowledge and Contextual Clues

Below are the sentences in which the vocabulary words appear in the text. Read the sentence. Use any clues you can find in the sentence combined with your prior knowledge, and write what you think the underlined words mean on the lines provided.

1. "I have no doubt they found my second appearance strange enough, coming suddenly out of the quiet darkness with <u>inarticulate</u> noises and the splutter and flare of a match."

    ____

2. "They came, and then, pointing to the bronze pedestal, I tried to <u>intimate</u> my wish to open it."

    ____

3. "Then I got a big pebble from the river, and came and hammered till I had flattened a coil in the decorations, and the <u>verdigris</u> came off in powdery flakes."

    ____

4. "Yet a certain feeling, you may understand, <u>tethered</u> me in a circle of a few miles round the point of my arrival."

    ____

5. "I must confess that my satisfaction with my first theories of an automatic civilisation and a <u>decadent</u> humanity did not long endure."

    ____

6. "I felt a peculiar shrinking from those <u>pallid</u> bodies. They were just the half-bleached colour of the worms and things one sees preserved in spirit in a zoological museum."

    ____

7. "Swinging myself in, I found it was the <u>aperture</u> of a narrow horizontal tunnel in which I could lie down and rest."

    ____

8. "Great shapes like big machines rose out of the dimness, and cast grotesque black shadows, in which dim <u>spectral</u> Morlocks sheltered from the glare."

    ____

9. "I determined to strike another match and escape under the protection of its glare. I did so, and <u>eking</u> out the flicker with a scrap of paper from my pocket, I made good my retreat to the narrow tunnel."

    ____

10. "That climb seemed <u>interminable</u> to me. With the last twenty or thirty feet of it a deadly nausea came upon me."

    ____

The Time Machine Vocabulary Worksheet Assignment 3 Continued

Part II: Determining the Meaning -- Match the vocabulary words to their dictionary definitions.

_____ 1.	INARTICULATE	A.	An opening, as a hole, slit, crack or gap
_____ 2.	INTIMATE	B.	Unending
_____ 3.	VERDIGRIS	C.	A blue-green crust formed on copper, brass, or bronze surfaces exposed to the atmosphere for long periods of time
_____ 4.	TETHERED	D.	To indicate or make known indirectly; hint; imply; suggest
_____ 5.	DECADENT	E.	Pale; faint or deficient in color
_____ 6.	PALLID	F.	Ghostly
_____ 7.	APERTURE	G.	Confined or restricted with or as if with a rope or chain
_____ 8.	SPECTRAL	H.	In a condition or process of mental or moral decay
_____ 9.	EKING	I.	Lacking the ability to express oneself, esp. in clear speech
_____ 10.	INTERMINABLE	J.	Getting with great effort or strain

Part I: Using Prior Knowledge and Contextual Clues

Below are the sentences in which the vocabulary words appear in the text. Read the sentence. Use any clues you can find in the sentence combined with your prior knowledge, and write what you think the underlined words mean on the lines provided.

1. "Hitherto I had merely thought myself <u>impeded</u> by the childish simplicity of the little people, and by some unknown forces which I had only to understand to overcome;..."

2. "In that darkling calm my senses seemed <u>preternaturally</u> sharpened."

3. "So we went down a long slope into a valley, and there in the dimness I almost walked into a little river.... Here too were <u>acacias</u>."

4. "I thought of the great <u>precessional</u> cycle that the pole of the earth describes."

5. "I felt assured now of what it was, and from the bottom of my heart I pitied this last feeble <u>rill</u> from the great flood of humanity."

6. "At first I was so much surprised by this ancient monument of an intellectual age, that I gave no thought to the possibilities it presented. Even my preoccupation about the Time Machine <u>receded</u> a little from my mind."

7. "But I could find no saltpeter; indeed, no nitrates of any kind. Doubtless they had <u>deliquesced</u> ages ago."

8. "I had judged the strength of the lever pretty correctly, for it snapped after a minute's strain, and I rejoined her with a <u>mace</u> in my hand more than sufficient, I judged, for any Morlock skull that I might encounter.

9. "I fancied at first that it was paraffin wax, and smashed the glass accordingly. But the odor of <u>camphor</u> was unmistakable. In the universal decay this volatile substance had chanced to survive...."

The Time Machine Vocabulary Worksheet Assignment 4 Continued

Part II: Determining the Meaning -- Match the vocabulary words to their dictionary definitions.

_____ 1. IMPEDED

    A. Out of the ordinary course of nature; exceptionally or abnormally

_____ 2. PRETERNATURALLY

    B. Fragrant yellow flowers used in making perfumes

_____ 3. ACACIAS

    C. Compound used in the manufacture of plastics and explosives

_____ 4. PRECESSIONAL

    D. Small brook; rivulet

_____ 5. RILL

    E. Became liquid by absorbing moisture from the air, as certain salts

_____ 6. RECEDED

    F. Moved away; retreated; withdrew

_____ 7. DELIQUESCED

    G. A club-like armor-breaking weapon of war

_____ 8. MACE

    H. The slow, conical motion of the earth's axis of rotation

_____ 9. CAMPHOR

    I. Slowed or obstructed the progress of

Part I: Using Prior Knowledge and Contextual Clues
    Below are the sentences in which the vocabulary words appear in the text. Read the sentence. Use any clues you can find in the sentence combined with your prior knowledge, and write what you think the underlined words mean on the lines provided.

1.   "Upon the shrubby hill of its edge Weena would have stopped, fearing the darkness before us; but a singular sense of impending <u>calamity</u>, that should indeed have served me as a warning, drove me onward."

    ____

2.   "I put Weena, still motionless, down upon a turfy <u>bole</u> and very hastily, as my first lump of camphor waned, I began collecting sticks and leaves."

    ____

3.   "I could feel the <u>succulent</u> giving of flesh and bone under my blows, and for a moment I was free."

    ____

4.   "Yet every now and then one would come straight towards me, setting loose a quivering horror that made me quick to <u>elude</u> him."

    ____

5.   "I cannot describe how it relieved me to think that it had escaped the awful fate to which it seemed destined. As I thought of that, I was almost moved to begin a massacre of the helpless <u>abominations</u> about me, but I contained myself."

    ____

6.   "And like blots upon the landscape rose the <u>cupolas</u> above the ways to the Under-world."

    ____

7.   "It is a law of Nature we overlook, that intellectual versatility is the <u>compensation</u> for change, danger, and trouble."

    ____

8.   "So here, after all my elaborate preparation for the siege of the White Sphinx, was a <u>meek</u> surrender."

    ____

9.   "Now as I stood and examined it, finding pleasure in the mere touch of the <u>contrivance</u>, the thing I had expected happened."

    ____

10. "I found myself in the same grey light and <u>tumult</u> I have already described."

    ____

The Time Machine Vocabulary Worksheet Assignment 5 Continued

Part II: Determining the Meaning -- Match the vocabulary words to their dictionary definitions.

____ 1.	CALAMITY	A.	Small domes set on a round base or resting on pillars
____ 2.	BOLE	B.	Avoid or escape by speed, cleverness, or trickery; to evade
____ 3.	SUCCULENT	C.	Full of juice; juicy
____ 4.	ELUDE	D.	Given or received in return for services, debt, injury, lack, etc.
____ 5.	ABOMINATIONS	E.	Great misfortune or disaster
____ 6.	CUPOLAS	F.	Things that cause a sense of disgust
____ 7.	COMPENSATION	G.	Overly submissive or compliant; spiritless; tame
____ 8.	MEEK	H.	Stem or trunk of a tree
____ 9.	CONTRIVANCE	I.	A device or control that is very useful for a particular job
____ 10.	TUMULT	J.	Highly distressing agitation of mind or feeling

Part I: Using Prior Knowledge and Contextual Clues
Below are the sentences in which the vocabulary words appear in the text. Read the sentence. Use any clues you can find in the sentence combined with your prior knowledge, and write what you think the underlined words mean on the lines provided.

1. "The palpitating grayness grew darker; then--though I was still travelling with <u>prodigious</u> velocity- the blinking succession of day and night, which was usually indicative of a slower pace, returned, and grew more and more marked."

____

2. "The sea stretched away to the south-west, to rise into a sharp, bright horizon against the <u>wan</u> sky."

____

3. "Its evil eyes were wriggling on their stalks, its mouth was all alive with appetite, and its vast ungainly claws, smeared with an <u>algal</u> slime, were descending upon me."

____

4. "As I stood sick and confused I saw again the moving thing upon the <u>shoal</u>--there was no mistake now that it was a moving thing--against the red water of the sea."

____

5. "Presently, when the million dial was at zero, I <u>slackened</u> speed."

____

6. "Presently I got up and came through the passage here, limping, because my heel was still painful, and feeling sorely <u>begrimed</u>."

____

7. I shared a cab with the Editor. He thought the tale a "<u>gaudy</u> lie." For my own part, I was unable to come to a conclusion.

____

8. As I took hold of the handle of the door I heard an exclamation, oddly <u>truncated</u> at the end, and a click and a thud.

____

9. I seemed to see a ghostly, indistinct figure sitting in a whirling mass of black and brass for a moment--a figure so transparent that the bench behind with its sheets of drawings was absolutely distinct; but this <u>phantasm</u> vanished as I rubbed my eyes.

____

10. It may be that he swept back into the past, and fell among the blood-drinking, hairy savages of the Age of Unpolished Stone; into the abysses of the Cretaceous Sea; or among the grotesque <u>saurians</u>, the huge reptilian brutes of the Jurassic times.

____

Part II: Determining the Meaning -- Match the vocabulary words to their dictionary definitions.

____ 1.	PRODIGIOUS	A.	Brilliantly or excessively showy
____ 2.	WAN	B.	Dirty
____ 3.	ALGAL	C.	Sandbank or sand bar in a body of water exposed at low tide
____ 4.	SHOAL	D.	Unnatural or sickly pallor; pallid; lacking color
____ 5.	SLACKENED	E.	Lizards or similar reptiles
____ 6.	BEGRIMED	F.	Shortened by or as if by having a part cut off; cut short
____ 7.	GAUDY	G.	Creation of the imagination or fancy; fantasy
____ 8.	TRUNCATED	H.	Extraordinary in size, amount, extent, degree, force, etc.
____ 9.	PHANTASM	I.	Relating to algae
____ 10.	SAURIANS	J.	Made or became slower; slowed down

	1	2	3	4	5	6
1	F	I	I	I	E	H
2	B	B	D	A	H	D
3	J	E	C	B	C	I
4	H	A	G	H	B	C
5	C	C	H	D	F	J
6	D	G	E	F	A	B
7	A	D	A	E	D	A
8	E	H	F	G	G	F
9	G	F	J	C	I	G
10	I	J	B		J	E

DAILY LESSONS

<u>Objectives</u>
1. To become familiar with the elements of the Science Fiction genre of literature
2. To hear the poem, "When I Heard the Learn'd Astronomer" by Walt Whitman as an introduction to the science fiction genre
3. To be introduced to H. G. Wells and his novel *The Time Machine*
4. To preview the vocabulary worksheet and study guide questions for Chapters 1-2
5. To read Chapters 1-2

<u>Activity #1</u>
Ask students to brainstorm what makes a good science fiction story; they should list at least three elements that should be included. Invite students to share their ideas aloud, and write them on the board. For any of the elements students may have missed (see list below), ask leading questions so they can come up with the answers themselves.

Damon Knight, author, editor, critic, and founder of the Science Fiction Writers of America, once attempted to quantify the elements of science fiction. He came up with the following list derived from a number of previously published formal definitions of science fiction.
* Science: using present factual information and projecting the outcomes of its use in future situations

* Technology and invention

* The future and the remote past, including all time travel stories

* Extrapolation: the process of imagining relatively probable worlds of the future by utilizing logical extensions of scientific and cultural curves and trends

* Scientific method

* Other places: planets, dimensions, etc., including visitors from above

* Catastrophes: natural or manmade

<u>Activity #2</u>
Give brief notes about the life of H. G. Wells (see introductory materials for this LitPlan), and discuss how certain aspects of his life and the changing world around him in the 19th Century might have lead him to write in the Science Fiction genre.

<u>Activity #3</u>
Read aloud the poem "When I Heard the Learn'd Astromomer" by Walt Whitman.
Since the poem is in public domain, a copy is included in this LitPlan. Have students answer the reading questions, and then discuss what elements of (or feelings about) the science fiction genre from the front board can be found in this poem.

<u>Activity #4</u>
Distribute the materials students will use in this unit. Explain in detail how students are to use these materials.

<u>Study Guides</u>   Students should read the study guide questions for each reading assignment prior to beginning the reading assignment to get a feeling for what events and ideas are important in the

section they are about to read. After reading the section, students will (as a class or individually) answer the questions to review the important events and ideas from that section of the novel. Students should keep the study guides as study materials for the unit test. **Review the study questions for Assignment #1 while you are looking at the study guides.**

Vocabulary   Prior to each reading assignment, students will do vocabulary work related to the section of the novel they are about to read. Following the completion of the reading of the novel, there will be a vocabulary review of all the words used in the vocabulary assignments. Students should keep their vocabulary work as study materials for the unit test. **Do the vocabulary worksheet for Assignment #1 together orally to show students how to do the vocabulary worksheets.**

Reading Assignment Sheet   You need to fill in the reading assignment sheet to let students know by when their reading has to be completed. You can either copy the assignments from the sheet onto a side blackboard or bulletin board and leave it there for students to see each day, or you can photocopy schedules for each student to have. In either case, you should advise students to become very familiar with the reading assignments so they know what is expected of them.

Extra Activities Center   The Unit Resource Materials portion of this LitPlan contains suggestions for an extra library of related boooks and articles in your classroom as well as crossword and word search puzzles. Make an extra activities center in your room where you will keep these materials for students to use. (Bring books and articles in from the library and keep several copies of the puzzles on hand). Explain to students that these materials are available for students to use when they finish reading assignments or other class work early.

Non-fiction Assignment Sheet   Explain to students that they each are to read at least one non-fiction piece from the in-class library at some time during the unit. Students will fill out a Non-fiction Assignment Sheet after completing the reading to help you (the teacher) evaluate their reading experiences and to help the students think about and evaluate their own reading experiences.

Books   Each school has its own rules and regulations regarding student use of school books. Advise students of the procedures that are normal for your school. Preview the book. Look at the covers, front-matter, and index.

Activity #5
Students should read Chapters 1-2 prior to the next class meeting. If time remains in this class, they may begin this assignment.

When I heard the learn'd astronomer,
When the proofs, the figures, were ranged in columns before me,
When I was shown the charts and diagrams, to add, divide, and measure them,
When I, sitting, heard the astronomer, where he lectured with much applause in the lecture room,
How soon, unaccountable, I became tired and sick,
Till rising and gliding out, I wander'd off by myself,
In the mystical mist night-air, and from time to time,
Look'd up in perfect silence at the stars.

Walt Whitman (1865, 1867)

1. What is the attitude of the Learn'd Astronomer regarding his scientific
   discoveries?

2. What is the narrator's attitude toward the Learn'd Astronomer (or scientific
   discovery in general)?

3. Why does the narrator, after wandering off by himself, look "up in perfect
   silence at the stars?" What does this say about him?

LESSON TWO

<u>Objectives</u>
1. To review the main events, ideas, and vocabulary from Chapters 1-2
2. To be able to demonstrate reading comprehension through sharing responses to study guide questions
3. To begin reading non-fiction articles relating to 19th Century scientific discoveries and relate them to *The Time Machine*
4. To practice research skills in the Library/Media Center
5. To preview the study guide questions and vocabulary for Chapters 3-4
6. To read Chapters 3-4

<u>Activity #1</u>
Give students a few minutes to formulate answers for the study guide questions for Chapters 1-2, and then discuss the answers to the questions in detail. Write the answers on the board or overhead transparency so students can have the correct answers for study purposes.

While students have their study guides out, preview the questions for Chapters 3-4.

NOTE: It is a good practice in public speaking and leadership skills for individual students to take charge of leading the discussions of the study questions. Perhaps a different student could go to the front of the class and lead the discussion each day that the study questions are discussed in this unit. Of course, you should guide the discussion when appropriate and try to fill in any gaps students may leave. The study questions could really be handled in a number of different ways, including in small groups with group reports following. Occasionally you may want to use the multiple choice questions as quizzes to check students' reading comprehension. As a short review now and then, students could pair up for the first (or last, if you have time left at the end of a class period) few minutes of class to quiz each other from the study questions. Mix up methods of reviewing the materials and checking comprehension throughout the unit so students don't get bored just answering the questions the same way each day. Variety in methods will also help address the different learning styles of your students. From now on in this unit, the directions will simply say, "Discuss the answers to the study questions in detail as previously directed." You will choose the method of preparation and discussion each day based on what best suits you and your class.

<u>Activity #2</u>
Review the vocabulary for Chapters 1-2. Be sure students write down the correct answers.

<u>Activity #3</u>
Take students to the Library/Media Center. Distribute the Non-fiction Reading Assignment and discuss the directions in detial. Each student will complete the Non-fiction Reading Assignment Sheet based on his/her particular articles he/she finds in the Library/Media Center that pertain to the topic of scientific discoveries of the 19th Century. Try to encourage each student to choose a different topic.

Students will share their findings on Day 6 and relate them to *The Time Machine*.

<u>Activity #4</u>
Instruct students to complete the vocabulary worksheet for Chapters 3-4 and to read those chapters prior to the next class meeting.

In H. G. Wells's science fiction novel, a man devotes his work and energy to the pursuit of a scientific experiment; he wants to travel in time. During the 19th Century, scientific discoveries and new ideas for looking at the world were emerging, and many authors of that time period were inspired to build stories surrounding these advancements.

Your task is to research scientific discoveries and new ideas that emerged during the mid-to-late 19th Century. Concentrate on one idea in particular, and explain how that discovery might have had an impact upon stories created by science fiction authors.

Example from the EARLY 19th Century:
Alchemists were fascinated with the thought that they might be able to create an elixir that would either prolong life, or regenerate dead tissue. This concept was reflected in Mary Shelley's *Frankenstein*, and as outlandish as the idea seemed at the time, today's medical practitioners routinely perform organ transplants in order to rejuvenate "dead" patients.

NON-FICTION ASSIGNMENT SHEET
(To be completed after reading the required non-fiction article)

Name _________________________________ Date _______________________________

Title of Non-fiction Read ____

Written By _______________________ Publication Date _________________________

I. Factual Summary: Write a short summary of the piece you read.

II. Vocabulary
    1. With which vocabulary words in the piece did you encounter some degree of difficulty?

    2. How did you resolve your lack of understanding with these words?

III. Interpretation: What was the main point the author wanted you to get from reading his work?

IV. Criticism
    1. With which points of the piece did you agree or find easy to accept? Why?

    2. With which points of the piece did you disagree or find difficult to believe? Why?

V. Personal Response: What do you think about this piece? <u>OR</u> How does this piece influence your ideas?

58

LESSON THREE

<u>Objectives</u>
1. To review the main events, ideas, and vocabulary from Chapters 3-4
2. To demonstrate reading comprehension through taking a quiz
3. To practice oral reading skills
4. To preview the study guide questions and vocabulary for Chapters 5-6
5. To read Chapters 5-6

<u>Activity #1</u>
Discuss the answers to the study questions for Chapters 3-4 as previously directed. While students have their study guides out, preview the questions for Chapters 5-6.

<u>Activity #2</u>
Quiz- Distribute quizzes for Chapters 1-4 and give students about 10 minutes to complete them.

After students have finished, have them exchange papers. Grade the quizzes as a class. Collect the papers for recording the grades.

<u>Activity #3</u>
Review the vocabulary for Chapters 3-4. Be sure students write down the correct answers. While students have their vocabulary worksheets out, do the worksheets for Chapters 5-6 orally together in class.

<u>Activity #4</u>
Read Chapters 5-6 of *The Time Machine* out loud in class. You probably know the best way to get readers with your class; pick students at random, ask for volunteers, or use whatever method works best for your group. If you have not yet completed an oral reading evaluation for your students this period, this would be a good opportunity to do so. A form is included with this unit for your convenience. If you don't finish this assignment in class, remind students that it should be completed prior to the next class.

1. According to the Time Traveller, what four extensions must any real body have in order to exist?
   A. Length, breadth, thickness, and duration
   B. Height, width, volume, and velocity
   C. Light, sound, weight, and opaqueness
   D. Length, breadth, thickness, and weight

2. How does the Time Traveller intend to prove his theory of time travel?
   A. He is going to synchronize his watch with the gentlemen's watches and then travel ten minutes into the future.
   B. He has created a small model of his Time Machine to show the men how it works.
   C. He intends to bring items from the past into the present.
   D. He plans to send the Psychologist ten minutes into the future.

3. What do the men see when the Psychologist presses the lever on the Time Machine model?
   A. The model disappears before their eyes.
   B. The Time Machine explodes in a cloud of smoke.
   C. The Psychologist disappears before their eyes.
   D. Nothing happens.

4. The Time Traveller is late for the second dinner party. What is in the note he left for the Medical Man?
   A. The Time Traveller instructs the Medical Man to begin dinner promptly at 7:00.
   B. The Time Traveller instructs the Medical Man to meet him at his laboratory at precisely 6:48 P.M.
   C. The Time Traveller instructs the Medical Man to use the time machine to join him in the future.
   D. The Time Traveller instructs the Medical Man to contact the police if he is more than one hour late for dinner.

5. Who seems to become the most nervous when the Time Traveller sits down to dinner?
   A. The Silent Man
   B. The Narrator
   C. The Medical Man
   D. The Psychologist

6. What prohibits the Time Traveller from using his machine as he had planned?
    A. He is afraid to use the machine because he doesn't know if he will survive the trip.
    B. He discovers the machine does not work, and he has to rebuild it.
    C. He is suffering from a terrible fever that has lasted for five days.
    D. One of the nickel bars is too short and has to be replaced.

7. What does the Time Traveller fear will happen if he stops the machine?
    A. He is afraid he will never return to his own time period.
    B. He is afraid he will not be able to find the fuel needed to run the machine.
    C. He is afraid he will blow up into the unknown.
    D. He is afraid the machine will not stop at all.

8. What does the Time Traveller do when the little people attempt to explore the machine?
    A. He unscrews the levers that make the machine work and puts them in his pocket.
    B. He yells and waves them away from the machine.
    C. He distracts their attention by walking away from the machine.
    D. He gets back in the machine and leaves.

9. How does the Time Traveller describe the little people who come to greet him?
    A. They are small with curly hair, bright lips, pointed chins, and mild eyes.
    B. They are small with long straight hair, pale lips, and wild eyes.
    C. They are extremely tall and bronze with superhuman strength.
    D. They are pale-complexioned with flaxen hair and greyish-red eyes.

10. Which best describes the land of the little people?
    A. It is a huge desert with a mountain range in the far distance.
    B. The land is filled with green plants and trees, huge amounts of flowers, and there are ruins in the distance.
    C. The natural landscape is masked by huge glass buildings and extensive roads.
    D. It is a vast wasteland.

A 1.   According to the Time Traveller, what four extensions must any real body have in order to exist?

    A. Length, breadth, thickness, and duration

    B. Height, width, volume, and velocity

    C. Light, sound, weight, and opaqueness

    D. Length, breadth, thickness, and weight

B 2.   How does the Time Traveller intend to prove his theory of time travel?

    A. He is going to synchronize his watch with the gentlemen's watches and then travel ten minutes into the future.

    B. He has created a small model of his Time Machine to show the men how it works.

    C. He intends to bring items from the past into the present.

    D. He plans to send the Psychologist ten minutes into the future.

A 3.   What do the men see when the Psychologist presses the lever on the Time Machine model?

    A. The model disappears before their eyes.

    B. The Time Machine explodes in a cloud of smoke.

    C. The Psychologist disappears before their eyes.

    D. Nothing happens.

A 4.   The Time Traveller is late for the second dinner party. What is in the note he left for the Medical Man?

    A. The Time Traveller instructs the Medical Man to begin dinner promptly at 7:00.

    B. The Time Traveller instructs the Medical Man to meet him at his laboratory at precisely 6:48 P.M.

    C. The Time Traveller instructs the Medical Man to use the time machine to join him in the future.

    D. The Time Traveller instructs the Medical Man to contact the police if he is more than one hour late for dinner.

A 5.   Who seems to become the most nervous when the Time Traveller sits down to dinner?

    A. The Silent Man

    B. The Narrator

    C. The Medical Man

    D. The Psychologist

D 6.   What prohibits the Time Traveller from using his machine as he had planned?
   A. He is afraid to use the machine because he doesn't know if he will survive the trip.
   B. He discovers the machine does not work, and he has to rebuild it.
   C. He is suffering from a terrible fever that has lasted for five days.
   D. One of the nickel bars is too short and has to be replaced.

C 7.   What does the Time Traveller fear will happen if he stops the machine?
   A. He is afraid he will never return to his own time period.
   B. He is afraid he will not be able to find the fuel needed to run the machine.
   C. He is afraid he will blow up into the unknown.
   D. He is afraid the machine will not stop at all.

A 8.   What does the Time Traveller do when the little people attempt to explore the machine?
   A. He unscrews the levers that make the machine work and puts them in his pocket.
   B. He yells and waves them away from the machine.
   C. He distracts their attention by walking away from the machine.
   D. He gets back in the machine and leaves.

A 9.   How does the Time Traveller describe the little people who come to greet him?
   A. They are small with curly hair, bright lips, pointed chins, and mild eyes.
   B. They are small with long straight hair, pale lips, and wild eyes.
   C. They are extremely tall and bronze with superhuman strength.
   D. They are pale-complexioned with flaxen hair and greyish-red eyes.

B 10.   Which best describes the land of the little people?
   A. It is a huge desert with a mountain range in the far distance.
   B. The land is filled with green plants and trees, huge amounts of flowers, and there are ruins in the distance.
   C. The natural landscape is masked by huge glass buildings and extensive roads.
   D. It is a vast wasteland.

ORAL READING EVALUATION - *The Time Machine*

Name _______________________ Class____ Date _________

SKILL	EXCELLENT	GOOD	AVERAGE	FAIR	POOR
Fluency	5	4	3	2	1
Clarity	5	4	3	2	1
Audibility	5	4	3	2	1
Pronunciation	5	4	3	2	1
____________	5	4	3	2	1
____________	5	4	3	2	1

Total _____   Grade _____

Comments:

LESSON FOUR

<u>Objectives</u>
1. To review the main events, ideas, and vocabulary from Chapters 5-6
2. To demonstrate an understanding of the difference between a physical characteristic and a character trait
3. To demonstrate an understanding of characterization through the creation of character journals
4. To improve cooperative learning skills through working in groups
5. To practice speaking in front of a group through the presentation of character journals
6. To practice note-taking skills while listening to others' presentations
7. To preview the study guide questions and vocabulary for Chapters 7-8
8. To read Chapters 7-8

<u>Activity #1</u>
Discuss the answers to the study guide questions for Chapters 5-6 as previously directed. While students have their study guides out, preview the questions for Chapters 7-8.

<u>Activity #2</u>
Review the vocabulary answers for Chapters 5-6.

<u>Activity #3</u>
Divide students into 6 groups. Ask two groups of students to come up with at least three positive character traits for the Time Traveller using textual support as evidence. Ask two other groups of students to come up with three negative character traits for the Time Traveller and supply textual evidence to support each trait. The remaining two groups will provide a physical description of the Time Traveller: one group will focus on the first night the Time Traveller met with the group of men, and the remaining group will focus on the night the Time Traveller was late for dinner.

When they have completed this task (usually about ten minutes), ask the groups to present the information. Those students who are listening must take notes on what they hear.

<u>Activity #4</u>
Assign each of the 6 groups one of the following: the Narrator, the Medical Man, the Psychologist, the Editor, the Journalist, and the Silent Man. Each pair/group will be given a large sheet of construction paper to be used to create a character poster. On each poster, the groups must provide the following:

* The name of the character (if it can be discerned from the text; most can), as well as his occupation

* A labeled picture of the character based on the physical description given in the text (labels should contain page numbers as evidence)

* At least two positive character traits with supporting evidence and corresponding page numbers for each

* At least two negative character traits with supporting evidence and corresponding page numbers for each

* Speculations as to why this particular person was invited to the dinner party by the Time Traveller

Each student is to create a journal entry that reflects this character's reaction to the Time Traveller's claims about his machine.

Activity #5
Have each group present its poster, speculations, and journal entries to the class while the rest of the class takes characterization notes.

Activity #6
Instruct students to complete the vocabulary worksheet for Chapters 7-8 and to read those chapters prior to the next class meeting.

LESSON FIVE

<u>Objectives</u>
1. To review the main events, ideas, and vocabulary from Chapters 7-8
2. To demonstrate reading comprehension through taking a quiz
3. To practice research skills
4. To work in cooperative groups
5. To practice writing to inform
6. To preview the study guide questions and vocabulary for Chapters 9-10
7. To read Chapters 9-10

<u>Activity #1</u>
Discuss the answers to the study questions for Chapters 7-8 as previously directed. While students have their study questions out, preview the questions for Chapters 9-10.

<u>Activity #2</u>
Quiz- Distribute quizzes for Chapters 5-8 and give students about 10 minutes to complete them.

When students finish, have them exchange papers. Grade the quizzes as a class. Collect the papers for recording the grades.

<u>Activity #3</u>
Review the answers to the vocabulary worksheet for Chapters 7-8.

<u>Activity #4</u>
Assign students to groups of three or four and distribute Writing Assignment #1. Each group of students will be selecting an author who wrote short stories in the science fiction genre. (You may use science fiction novels if you have the time to devote to a long term project.) Each student within the group will select a different story by that particular author, and each individual will write an essay exploring the elements of science fiction as discussed in the first lesson. As a group, the students will make a poster devoted to their author, as well as research his/her life for ideas that might explain why he/she decided to write in this genre. Also, students will explore events in the scientific world that may have had an impact upon each of the short stories. Students will give a presentation at the end of the unit.

<u>Activity #5</u>
Take students to the Library/Media Center to begin their research.

<u>Activity #6</u>
Instruct students to complete the vocabulary worksheets for Chapters 9-10 and to read those chapters prior to the next class meeting.

1. What does the Time Traveller discover when he returns to the area surrounding the White Sphinx on the first night?
    A. He finds a young boy examining the Time Machine closely.
    B. Someone has smashed the dials of the Time Machine.
    C. He discovers the Time Machine is gone.
    D. The statue of the White Sphinx has been beheaded.

2. Although he is in great distress over the missing Time Machine, what one fact makes the Time Traveller feel reassured?
    A. He has the plans to the machine in his pocket and can build a new machine.
    B. He has the levers to work the machine in his pocket.
    C. He knew even if he could not get home, he would be very happy living with the little people.
    D. He has the key to start the machine in his pocket.

3. When the Time Traveller goes to the second great hall trying to find the Time Machine, what item does he use that the little people have forgotten?
    A. Matches
    B. Magnifying glasses
    C. Scissors
    D. Eye glasses

4. How do the Time Traveller and Weena become friends?
    A. He asks her to serve as a guide into the wilderness as he looks for his Time Machine.
    B. Weena's father gives her to the Time Traveller as a gift.
    C. The Time Traveller saves her from drowning.
    D. Weena feels pity for him because he is alone, so she hangs out with him.

5. What does the Time Traveller learn about the diet of the Morlocks?
    A. They only eat once a week.
    B. They are vegetarians.
    C. They are carnivores.
    D. They eat the rodents that live in their caves.

6.	Why does the Time Traveller regard the new moon as his enemy?
     A.	With every passing of the new moon an Eloi must be given to the Morlocks.
     B.	He dreads the darkness of the new moon because the Morlocks come out in the dark.
     C.	He dreads the darkness of the new moon because he is running out of matches.
     D.	With every passing of the new moon the Time Traveller fears he will never return home again.

7.	What souvenir from the future world does the Time Traveller remove from his pocket to show his dinner guests?
     A.	A lump of camphor
     B.	A necklace made by Weena
     C.	A box of matches
     D.	Two wilted flowers

8.	What confuses the Time Traveller about the stars?
     A.	He tries to find the North Star but can not determine which one it is.
     B.	The familiar constellations are no longer in the sky.
     C.	There are no stars in the sky.
     D.	They are so close to the earth that they reflect light, even at nighttime.

9.	What is the Palace of Green Porcelain?
     A.	It is the Time Traveller's own house.
     B.	It is an ancient museum.
     C.	It is an ancient bank.
     D.	It is an ancient train station.

10.	After finding a block of sulphur in one of the galleries, what idea sets the Time Traveller's mind racing?
     A.	He wonders if he can find the proper ingredients to make gunpowder.
     B.	He can place the lighted sulphur blocks at the openings of the Morlock caves to keep them in at night.
     C.	He can use all the blocks he's found to create a stronghold for himself.
     D.	He believes the terrible smell of sulphur burning will keep the Morlocks away.

C 1. What does the Time Traveller discover when he returns to the area surrounding the White Sphinx on the first night?
   A. He finds a young boy examining the Time Machine closely.
   B. Someone has smashed the dials of the Time Machine.
   C. He discovers the Time Machine is gone.
   D. The statue of the White Sphinx has been beheaded.

B 2. Although he is in great distress over the missing Time Machine, what one fact makes the Time Traveller feel reassured?
   A. He has the plans to the machine in his pocket and can build a new machine.
   B. He has the levers to work the machine in his pocket.
   C. He knew even if he could not get home, he would be very happy living with the little people.
   D. He has the key to start the machine in his pocket.

A 3. When the Time Traveller goes to the second great hall trying to find the Time Machine, what item does he use that the little people have forgotten?
   A. Matches
   B. Magnifying glasses
   C. Scissors
   D. Eye glasses

C 4. How do the Time Traveller and Weena become friends?
   A. He asks her to serve as a guide into the wilderness as he looks for his Time Machine.
   B. Weena's father gives her to the Time Traveller as a gift.
   C. The Time Traveller saves her from drowning.
   D. Weena feels pity for him because he is alone, so she hangs out with him.

C 5. What does the Time Traveller learn about the diet of the Morlocks?
   A. They only eat once a week.
   B. They are vegetarians.
   C. They are carnivores.
   D. They eat the rodents that live in their caves.

B 6. Why does the Time Traveller regard the new moon as his enemy?

  A. With every passing of the new moon an Eloi must be given to the Morlocks.

  B. He dreads the darkness of the new moon because the Morlocks come out in the dark.

  C. He dreads the darkness of the new moon because he is running out of matches.

  D. With every passing of the new moon the Time Traveller fears he will never return home again.

D 7. What souvenir from the future world does the Time Traveller remove from his pocket to show his dinner guests?

  A. A lump of camphor

  B. A necklace made by Weena

  C. A box of matches

  D. Two wilted flowers

B 8. What confuses the Time Traveller about the stars?

  A. He tries to find the North Star but can not determine which one it is.

  B. The familiar constellations are no longer in the sky.

  C. There are no stars in the sky.

  D. They are so close to the earth that they reflect light, even at nighttime.

B 9. What is the Palace of Green Porcelain?

  A. It is the Time Traveller's own house.

  B. It is an ancient museum.

  C. It is an ancient bank.

  D. It is an ancient train station.

A 10. After finding a block of sulphur in one of the galleries, what idea sets the Time Traveller's mind racing?

  A. He wonders if he can find the proper ingredients to make gunpowder.

  B. He can place the lighted sulphur blocks at the openings of the Morlock caves to keep them in at night.

  C. He can use all the blocks he's found to create a stronghold for himself.

  D. He believes the terrible smell of sulphur burning will keep the Morlocks away.

WRITING ASSIGNMENT #1 *The Time Machine*

<u>PROMPT</u>
The scientific ideas and discoveries in the late 19th century prompted many people to speculate on the question, "What if?" Authors in the science fiction genre attempted to answer this question by basing their tales on scientific evidence and letting their imaginations fly with the idea. This is a group writing assignment. Each group will select a different science fiction author as a focus of study. Each group must do all of the following:

1. Students will research biographical information about the author.

2. Each member will read a different short story written by the author and analyze it for its science fiction elements.

3. Each member will research information about scientific ideas during that author's lifetime that seem to be refected in the short story. (Your non-fiction assignments might be of help for this.)

4. Students will meet in their groups to compare notes and discuss the author and his/her works.

5. Students will create a group poster devoted to the author and his life/work.

6. Each member will write a report including: biography of author, summary of story's science fiction elements, applicable scientific ideas tied to story, and comments/conclusions from group discussion--common traits of author's works.

7. Each group will give a presentation at the end of the unit.

<u>PREWRITING</u>
After deciding on the author, read, highlight, and annotate the short story you will be using for your individual analysis essay for this project. You should highlight sections of the story that support specific elements of the science fiction genre, and any annotations should be an explanation of why you highlighted that particular section. You also need to make correlations to scientific discoveries/ideas that were prevalent during the time period in which the story was written, so you may have to do some research about that. Be sure to take accurate notes when researching.

<u>DRAFTING</u>
Your report will have sections as noted in the assignment prompt above. Be sure to use a variety of sentence structures and incorporate at least six vocabulary words in your report.

<u>PROMPT</u>
When you finish the rough draft of your report, ask a student whose opinions you trust to read it. After reading your rough draft, he/she should tell you what he/she liked best about your work, which parts were difficult to understand, and ways in which your work could be improved. Reread your paper considering your critic's comments, and make the corrections you think are necessary. Do a final proofreading of your paper, double-checking your grammar, spelling, organizaton, and the clarity of your ideas.

Name ____

Group's Author _______________________________________

Story Read ____

Notes About the Biography of the Author:

Summary of the Story's Science Fiction Elements:

Applicable Scientific Ideas Tied to the Story:

Comments/Conclusions From Group Discussion--Common Traits of Author's Works:

WRITING EVALUATION FORM - *The Time Machine*

Name ____ Date_____________Grade ____________

Circle One For Each Item:

Grammar:	correct	errors noted on paper
Spelling:	correct	errors noted on paper
Punctuation:	correct	errors noted on paper

Legibility: excellent   good   fair   poor

____________   excellent   good   fair   poor

____________   excellent   good   fair   poor

Strengths:

Weaknesses:

Comments/Suggestions:

LESSON SIX

<u>Objectives</u>
1. To review the main events, ideas, and vocabulary from Chapters 9-10
2. To check students' non-fiction reading assignments
3. To practice public speaking skills through an oral presentation
4. To connect 19th Century scientific discoveries to the novel
5. To preview the study guide questions and vocabulary for Chapters 11-12 and the Epilogue
6. To read Chapters 11-12 and the Epilogue

<u>Activity #1</u>
Discuss the answers to the study guide questions for Chapters 9-10 as previously directed. While students have their study guides out, preview the questions for Chapters 11-12 and the Epilogue.

<u>Activity #2</u>
Review vocabulary for Chapters 9-10. Be sure students write down the correct answers.

<u>Activity #3</u>
Ask each student to give a brief oral report about the non-fiction articles he/she read. Your criteria for evaluating this report will vary depending on the level of your students. You may wish for students to give a complete report without using notes of any kind, or you may want students to read directly from a written report, or you may want to do something in between these two extremes. Just make students aware of your criteria in ample time for them to prepare their reports.

Start with one student's report. Then, ask if anyone else in the class has read on a topic related to the first student's report. If so, go to that student's report. If no one has, choose another student at random. After each report, be sure to ask if anyone has a report related to the one just completed. That will help maintain continuity during the discussion about the information students have just shared.

<u>Activity #4</u>
If there is still time, allow groups to get together to work on their scientific fiction projects.

<u>Activity #5</u>
Instruct students to complete the vocabulary worksheets for Chapter 11 through the Epilogue and to read the remainder of the book prior to the next class meeting.

LESSON SEVEN

<u>Objectives</u>
1. To review the main events, ideas, and vocabulary from Chapters 11-12 and the Epilogue
2. To demonstrate reading comprehension through taking a quiz
3. To exercise logical thinking, particularly cause and effect relationships
4. To reflect on a problem from the past and create a viable solution
5. To express personal ideas in writing
6. To evaluate students' writing skills

<u>Activity #1</u>
Discuss the answers to the study questions for Chapters 11-12 and Epilogue as previously directed.

<u>Activity #2</u>
Quiz- Distribute quizzes for Chapters 9-the Epilogue and give students about 10 minutes to complete them. When all students are done, have them exchange papers. Grade quizzes as a class. Collect the papers for recording the grades.

<u>Activity #3</u>
Review the vocabulary for Chapters 11-12 and the Epilogue. Be sure students write down the correct answers.

<u>Activity #4</u>
Distribute Writing Assignment #2 and discuss the directions in detail. Students will write a reflection about something they wish they could go back and change (either in their personal life or an event in history). In the essay, they must describe the original history as well as what they think might need to be changed. However, since every action has a definite reaction, ask students to speculate about what future events might be impacted by this change. Is the change going to be for the best in the long run, or would it only fix a short term problem?

<u>Activity #5</u>
Students who complete the essay before the end of class may work on their science fiction project.

1. What does the Time Traveller do that he later discovers to be an "atrocious folly?"
   A. He lights the firewood to frighten the Morlocks.
   B. He runs into the woods without first checking his whereabouts.
   C. He throws the sticks of dynamite at the Morlocks.
   D. He leaves Weena unguarded near a hollow tree.

2. What is the source of the "slumberous murmur" the Time Traveller hears in the forest?
   A. It is the sound of the Time Traveller snoring.
   B. It is the sound of the only creature the Morlocks fear.
   C. It is the sound the Eloi make trying to scare the Morlocks.
   D. It is the sound of a forest fire roaring.

3. What does the Time Traveller notice about the Time Machine when he finds it?
   A. It is covered with a slimy film from being underground.
   B. The Morlocks have cleaned and oiled it thoroughly.
   C. The dials are broken; he doesn't know if the machine will work.
   D. The crystal that makes it work is now cracked.

4. The Time Traveller prepares to put the levers back into the machine, what "one little thing" does he realize he has overlooked?
   A. He can't start the machine until it is back in the exact spot where he arrived.
   B. He has left the matches outside.
   C. He has not fixed the broken lever.
   D. He can't light the matches without the match box.

5. How does the Time Traveller finally escape the Morlocks?
   A. He fights the Morlocks while he inserts the levers into the machine. He is able to turn it on and escape.
   B. The Eloi come to his rescue and distract the Morlocks long enough for him to leave.
   C. He throws a stick of dynamite at them and blows them up.
   D. He lures them to a tunnel he has filled with gunpowder. He then sets off the charge, sealing the Morlocks inside.

6.   What does the Time Traveller notice when he looks at the dials of the Time Machine after escaping the Morlocks?
   A.   The dials no longer work so he has no idea where he is going.
   B.   He realizes he forgot to set the dials for his own time period.
   C.   He notices he is traveling further into the future.
   D.   He notices he is traveling back to prehistoric times.

7.   The Time Traveller stops on a beach. What type of creatures surround the Time Machine?
   A.   They are super-humans who are able to read the Time Traveller's mind.
   B.   They are primitive humans in animal skins who do not possess language skills.
   C.   They are large crab-like creatures with claws, long antennae, and many legs.
   D.   They are small, football shaped creatures with slimy tentacles.

8.   When the Time Traveller returns home, why does the Time Machine land in a differnt place than it had left?
   A.   The velocity of passing time has propelled the machine physically forward.
   B.   It lands in a different spot because it had been moved by the Morlocks.
   C.   The orbit of the Earth has changed.
   D.   The machine skids to a stop when the Time Traveller lands.

9.   What does the Editor say after the Time Traveller completes his fantastic tale?
   A.   He says it's a pity the Time Traveller isn't a writer of stories.
   B.   He says the story must be kept secret from the citizens of the world.
   C.   He says he wants to start a committee to study the benefits of time travel.
   D.   He says the Time Traveller is crazy and insists on calling the authorities.

10.   What becomes of the Time Traveller?
   A.   He is committed to an insane asylum.
   B.   He is so traumatized by his experiences that he destroys the time machine.
   C.   He enters the time machine once more and is never seen again.
   D.   He becomes world-famous for his invention.

A 1.　What does the Time Traveller do that he later discovers to be an "atrocious folly?"

    A.　He lights the firewood to frighten the Morlocks.

    B.　He runs into the woods without first checking his whereabouts.

    C.　He throws the sticks of dynamite at the Morlocks.

    D.　He leaves Weena unguarded near a hollow tree.

D 2.　What is the source of the "slumberous murmur" the Time Traveller hears in the forest?

    A.　It is the sound of the Time Traveller snoring.

    B.　It is the sound of the only creature the Morlocks fear.

    C.　It is the sound the Eloi make trying to scare the Morlocks.

    D.　It is the sound of a forest fire roaring.

B 3.　What does the Time Traveller notice about the Time Machine when he finds it?

    A.　It is covered with a slimy film from being underground.

    B.　The Morlocks have cleaned and oiled it thoroughly.

    C.　The dials are broken; he doesn't know if the machine will work.

    D.　The crystal that makes it work is now cracked.

D 4.　The Time Traveller prepares to put the levers back into the machine, what "one little thing" does he realize he has overlooked?

    A.　He can't start the machine until it is back in the exact spot where he arrived.

    B.　He has left the matches outside.

    C.　He has not fixed the broken lever.

    D.　He can't light the matches without the match box.

A 5.　How does the Time Traveller finally escape the Morlocks?

    A.　He fights the Morlocks while he inserts the levers into the machine. He is able to turn it on and escape.

    B.　The Eloi come to his rescue and distract the Morlocks long enough for him to leave.

    C.　He throws a stick of dynamite at them and blows them up.

    D.　He lures them to a tunnel he has filled with gunpowder. He then sets off the charge, sealing the Morlocks inside.

C 6.   What does the Time Traveller notice when he looks at the dials of the Time Machine
        after escaping the Morlocks?
     A.   The dials no longer work so he has no idea where he is going.
     B.   He realizes he forgot to set the dials for his own time period.
     C.   He notices he is traveling further into the future.
     D.   He notices he is traveling back to prehistoric times.

C 7.   The Time Traveller stops on a beach. What type of creatures surround the Time
        Machine?
     A.   They are super-humans who are able to read the Time Traveller's mind.
     B.   They are primitive humans in animal skins who do not possess language skills.
     C.   They are large crab-like creatures with claws, long antennae, and many legs.
     D.   They are small, football shaped creatures with slimy tentacles.

B 8.   When the Time Traveller returns home, why does the Time Machine land in a differnt
        place than it had left?
     A.   The velocity of passing time has propelled the machine physically forward.
     B.   It lands in a different spot because it had been moved by the Morlocks.
     C.   The orbit of the Earth has changed.
     D.   The machine skids to a stop when the Time Traveller lands.

A 9.   What does the Editor say after the Time Traveller completes his fantastic tale?
     A.   He says it's a pity the Time Traveller isn't a writer of stories.
     B.   He says the story must be kept secret from the citizens of the world.
     C.   He says he wants to start a committee to study the benefits of time travel.
     D.   He says the Time Traveller is crazy and insists on calling the authorities.

C 10.   What becomes of the Time Traveller?
     A.   He is committed to an insane asylum.
     B.   He is so traumatized by his experiences that he destroys the time machine.
     C.   He enters the time machine once more and is never seen again.
     D.   He becomes world-famous for his invention.

PROMPT

Imagine that you have discovered a time machine of your very own. Instead of traveling into the future, however, you decide you would rather go back into the past to revisit a specific event and possibly change its outcome. One thing to keep in mind is that if one specific event is changed, it creates a domino effect that trickles down to the present.

PREWRITING

Decide upon an event in the past you wish to change. Using a graphic organizer, predict possible specific "trickle down effects" of making this change. Come up with at least three changes: two for the better, and one for the worse.

DRAFTING

After organizing your notes, write an essay that begins with the reason for going back in time. In your introduction, fully describe the situation, and explain what changes you wish to make. Be specific. You must then concentrate on the results of these actions, both positive and negative. Write two paragraphs, each explaining and supporting one positive effect of the change, and write one paragraph explaining and supporting one negative effect of the change. Use a variety of sentence structures (simple, compound, compound-complex) as well as incorporating at least five vocabulary words from the unit into your essay. Your concluding paragraphs should state whether or not the change would be worthwhile in light of the evidence you have given in your body paragraphs.

REVISING

When you finish the rough draft of your composition, ask a student whose opinions you trust to read it. After reading your rough draft, he/she should tell you what he/she liked best about your work, which parts were difficult to understand, and ways in which your work could be improved. Reread your paper considering your critic's comments, and make the corrections you think are necessary.

PROOFREADING

Do a final proofreading of your paper, double-checking your grammar, spelling, organization, and the clarity of your ideas.

LESSON EIGHT

<u>Objectives</u>
1. To demonstrate cooperative learning skills through working in groups
2. To practice writing skills throuh working on a writing assignment
3. To create the posters required for the science fiction group project
4. To prepare students for a discussion of the book *The Time Machine*

<u>Activity #1</u>
Choose the questions from the Extra Discussions/Writing Assignments which seem most appropriate for your students. A class discussion of these questions is most effective if students have been given the opportunity to formulate answers to the questions prior to the discussion. To this end, you may either have all the students formulate answers to all the questions, divide your class into groups and assign one or more questions to each group, or you could assign one question to each student in your class. The option you choose will make a difference in the amount of class time needed for this activity. The class discussion of these questions is scheduled for Lesson Ten. Tell students they should formulate answers to their assigned questions prior to Lesson Ten.

NOTE: The use of graphic organizers may be helpful to students in preparing their answers. Encourage them to use any diagrams or graphics that they feel are necessary.

<u>Activity #2</u>
Students will use the information they have gathered in their research and work in their Writing Assignment #1 groups to create the poster dedicated to their particular author. Each poster must contain the following:
  * The author's name

  * Dates of birth and death

  * A brief chronology of his/her life (important events)

  * The titles of the stories read by the group members

  * In the space by the title of the story, the science fiction elements found in the tale and the related scientific idea(s)

<u>Activity #3</u>
If students finish their posters prior to the end of class, they may work on their essays for the group project, edit/revise the essays from the previous class, or begin to work on formulating answers for their assigned discussion questions.

Interpretive

1. Discuss three specific character traits for the Time Traveller. Speculate as to why he seems so driven to travel into the future.

2. What seems to be the main conflict in H. G. Wells' *The Time Machine*? Fully describe the conflict and how it is (or is not) resolved.

3. How does the fact that a portion of the novel is set in 19th Century England play an important part in the events of the plot? What elements of life in the 19th Century seem to play a key role in the main conflict?

4. What elements of setting are important to the science fiction novel? How would the novel have been different if it had been set in the American Mid-West? The Far East? How might the setting have to be adjusted in order to maintain a sci-fi quality?

5. Examine the Time Traveller's guest list. Why do you suppose he invites these specific men to witness his achievement? Why don't most of the men take the Time Traveller seriously? What does this say about their characters?

6. H. G. Wells introduces The Silent Man who seems nervous at the dinner party, yet he never divulges the man's identity or his occupation. Speculate on who this man might be, and create a hypothesis as to why he is so nervous.

7. The Narrator seems to be the only man who believes the Time Traveller. What convinces him? Why does he keep the flowers from the Time Traveller's pocket? What do these actions say about the character of the Narrator?

8. Describe the climax of the novel.

Critical

9. Explain what caused the Morlocks to seek refuge beneath the ground. While underground, they maintain the technical aspects (machines, production of goods) that the present society views as "civilized," yet the Time Traveller is horrified by them. What horrifies him? What might H. G. Wells be saying about present society?

10. After seeing the horrors the future holds, why do you suppose the Time Traveller gets back in his machine?

11. Explain the symbolism of the wilted flowers. What do they mean to the Time Traveller? What do they mean to the Narrator?

12. What might be the motivation behind the Time Traveller's invention of the Time Machine in the first place? What does he hope to learn? Why might he have chosen to go into the future instead of going into the past?

13. H. G. Wells paints a bleak picture of the future of the earth and civilization. Why might he depict such a terrible projection? What might Wells be saying about tendencies in the behavior of the human race?

14. How does the seemingly Utopian society of the Eloi act as a source of irony in the novel? How about the Morlocks' caves?

15. Weena is the only Eloi given a name in the novel. How does the fact that the Time Traveller names her set her apart from the rest of society? How does the fact that she has a name make her death all the more tragic?

16. Consider the names of these characters: The Editor/Blank, The Journalist/Dash, The Silent Man/Chose and the housekeeper/Mrs. Watchett. How are these names a form of irony?

17. Why do you suppose H. G. Wells has his character travel into the future as opposed to going back into the past? How might the story have been different if this had been the case?

18. Compare the climate of present-day London with that of the London area in the future. How might the fact that the London area seemed to become a lush, warm climate reflect today's concern about global warming? Consider the irony of the fact that H. G. Wells wrote this novel in 1898, yet he depicts the warming of the climate in the future.

19. Suppose that Weena did not die in the fire as the Time Traveller supposes, and that she survived unbeknownst to him. How might the future of the Eloi have been different based on her interactions with him?

20. Suppose you had been invited to the Time Traveller's dinner party. What might have been your reaction to such an outlandish tale? Would you have told others about what you'd heard, or would you keep it to yourself? Explain your response.

Personal Response

21. Do you enjoy tales about the future? Why or why not? If you are one of those who is afraid of what the future might hold, explain what parts of *The Time Machine* scared you and why.

22. What age do you think is most appropriate for reading novels like *The Time Machine*? Explain why.

23. Do you intend to read more books from the science fiction genre? Why or why not?

24. Which of the characters do you identify with the most? Why?

<u>Objectives</u>
To review all of the vocabulary work done in this unit

<u>Activity</u>
Choose one (or more) of the vocabulary review activities listed below and spend your class period as directed in the activity. Some of the materials for these review activities are located in the Vocabulary Resource Materials section in the LitPlan.

VOCABULARY REVIEW ACTIVITIES

1. Divide your class into two teams and have an old fashioned spelling or definition bee.

2. Give each of your students (or students in groups of two, three or four) a *The Time Machine* Vocabulary Word Search Puzzle. The first person (group) to find all of the vocabulary words in the puzzle wins.

3. Give students a *The Time Machine* Vocabulary Word Search Puzzle without the word list. The person or group to find the most vocabulary words in the puzzle wins.

4. Use a *The Time Machine* Vocabulary Crossword Puzzle. Put the puzzle onto a transparency on the overhead projector (so everyone can see it), and do the puzzle together as a class.

5. Give students a *The Time Machine* Vocabulary Matching Worksheet to do.

6. Divide your class into two teams. Use *The Time Machine's* vocabulary words with their letters jumbled as a word list. Student 1 from Team A faces off against Student 1 from Team B. You write the first jumbled word on the board. The first student (1A or 1B) to unscramble the word wins the chance for his/her team to score points. If 1A wins the jumble, go to student 2A and give him/her a definition. He/she must give you the correct spelling of the vocabulary word which fits the definition. If he/she does, Team A scores a point, and you give student 3A a definition for which you expect a correctly spelled matching vocabulary word. Continue giving Team A definitions until some team member makes an incorrect response. An incorrect response sends the game back to the jumbled-word face off, this time with students 2A and 2B. Instead of repeating giving definitions to the first few students of each team, continue with the student after the one who gave the last incorrect response on the team. For example, if Team B wins the jumbled-word face-off, and student 5B gave the last incorrect answer for Team B, you would start this round of definition questions with student 6B, and so on. The team with the most points wins!

7. Have students write a story in which they correctly use as many vocabulary words as possible. Have students read their compositions orally! Post the most original compositions on your bulletin board.

8. Play *I Have, Who Has?* *NOTE: This requires preparation in advance. On 3x5 cards, write a vocabulary word on one side and a definition to another word on the other side of the card. Once you have completed a set, pass the cards out randomly, keeping one for yourself. You will start the game by saying, "Who has..." and reading the definition on the card. The student who has the word on his/her card that matches the definition shouts, "I have..." and reads the word. He/she then turns over the card and says, "Who has..." and play continues until all the words/cards have been gone through.

9. Divide the class into two teams and play Baseball. The "pitcher" reads the definition of a word and in order to get a "hit" the "batter" must give the correct word to match the definition. For this game, though, only one strike is allowed! If the "batter" gives the correct word, he/she moves to first base and the next "batter" comes up for another word. Score is kept like baseball with three outs and then the teams switch places.

LESSON TEN

<u>Objectives</u>
1. To demonstrate an understanding of the novel beyond the factual questions asked in the study guide
2. To practice public speaking skills through sharing answers to discussion questions

<u>Activity</u>
Students will share responses to the Extra Discussion Questions assigned during Lesson Eight. All students should take notes during the discussion.

LESSON ELEVEN

<u>Objectives</u>
1. To demonstrate their writing skills through the completion of an in-class writing assignment
2. To demonstrate the ability to work independently

<u>Activity #1</u>
Distribute the Writing Assignment #3 to each student and discuss the directions in detail. Give students the remaining time to write the essay in class.

<u>Activity #2</u>
Any student who finishes his/her essay before the end of class may work on other writing assignments.

PROMPT
You will read four quotations and select one you feel best supports the main idea of H. G. Wells's *The Time Machine*. In your essay, you need to indicate whether or not you agree with the main idea of the quotation and then defend your position by using specific textual support from *The Time Machine*.

PREWRITING
Choose one of the following:

History is moving, and it will tend toward hope, or tend toward tragedy.
 -George W. Bush

If knowledge can create problems, it is not through ignorance that we can solve them.
 -Isaac Asimov

The more rapidly a civilization progresses, the sooner it dies for another to rise in its place.
 -Havelock Ellis

Civilization begins with order, grows with liberty, and dies with chaos.
 -Will Durant

Decide whether or not you agree with the main idea of your selected quotation and choose specific textual evidence from *The Time Machine* that best supports your position.

DRAFTING
In your introduction, explain the meaning of the selected quotation and state whether or not you agree with the speaker (without using the first person). This is best done by indicating whether or not the statement is true. At the end of your introduction, create a thesis statement in which you refer to H. G. Wells' novel as support for your position. Your body paragraphs should contain at least two specific scenes from *The Time Machine* (complete with embedded quotations and parenthetical citations) that support your position on the quotation. Conclude your essay with some sort of a challenge to your reader with reference to the quotation.

REVISING
When you finish the rough draft of your paper, set it aside to bring to the next class for a peer-edit. After reading your rough draft, your editor will tell you what he/she liked best about your work, which parts were difficult to understand, and ways in which your work could be improved. Reread your paper considering your critic's comments, respond to the comments on the editing sheet, and make the corrections you think are necessary.

PROOFREADING
Do a final proofreading of your paper, double checking your grammar, spelling, organization, and the clarity of your ideas.

<u>Objectives</u>
1. To demonstrate students' abilities to assess another's writing through a peer editing exercise
2. To demonstrate students' abilities to accept constructive criticism and make changes in their writing when necessary

<u>Activity #1</u>
Put students in pairs for peer editing and give each student a Peer Evaluation Form. Students will exchange their persuasive essays written in class the day before and make comments regarding content, language use, and conventions (under "Editor"). Students will return the essays to the writer and then they respond to their peers' comments about their own writing on the editing sheet (under "Writer"). After thanking his/her peer for his/her comments, the writer will revise and rewrite the essay to turn in for a grade.

<u>Activity #2</u>
When students have edited and revised their writing and turned the essays in to be graded, they may work on finishing their projects for the upcoming presentations.

Editor's Name ____ Date _______________

Writer's Name ____Assignment______________

Peer Editing for Writing Assignments

A. Was the writer's position clearly stated?

If your answer is "yes," be sure to tell the writer what he/she did that you especially liked. If your answer is "no," tell the writer what he/she could have included in order to write a better essay.

*Editor:*____

____

____

Writer: ____

____

____

B. Did he/she provide enough details to support his/her position?

If your answer is "yes," be sure to tell the writer what you especially liked about his/her response. If your answer is "no," you must tell the writer how he/she could improve his/her response (adding specific details that were missed, connecting to position better, or adding embedded quotations).

*Editor:*____

____

____

Writer: ____

____

____

C. Identify sentence type

Be sure to know the difference between simple, simple with compound subject, simple with compound predicate, compound, complex, and compound-complex. Using the first body paragraph, correctly identify each sentence type. If there is sufficient sentence structure variety, tell the writer what he/she did well. If not, explain what he/she could have done differently.

Sentence 1: ________________________	*Sentence 5:* ________________________
Sentence 2: ________________________	*Sentence 6:* ________________________
Sentence 3: ________________________	*Sentence 7:* ________________________
Sentence 4: ________________________	*Sentence 8:* ________________________

*Editor:*____

____

____

____

*Writer:*____

____

____

D. Address the Focus Correction Areas

Did the writer follow the specifics of the essay such as (address each individually):

Organization:

Editor: ____

Writer: ____

Use of Vocabulary as Directed:

Editor: ____

Writer: ____

Citations from novel as support:

Editor: ____

Writer: ____

E. Check for Errors in Punctuation, Grammar, Spelling, etc.

Editor: ____

Writer: ____

Comments:

LESSONS THIRTEEN AND FOURTEEN

<u>Objectives</u>
1. To practice public speaking skills through presentation of science fiction projects
2. To improve listening skills through listening to class presentations
3. To demonstrate questioning skills through the formulation of a question and answer session about each story and/or author

<u>Activity #1</u>
Students will present their group projects about science fiction authors. Discuss the author first, and then each student will present his/her sci-fi story and analysis. A form for group assessment follows. After each group has presented, audience members may question group members about the author or any of the stories for clarification.

<u>Activity #2</u>
If all groups finish with presentations before time is up, students may participate in more of the vocabulary review lessons or look ahead to the review materials for Lesson Sixteen.

Group Presentation Evaluation Sheet

Each of the following will be graded on a scale of 1-5, with 1 being the lowest; each is worth 20% of the overall grade.

Part I: individual contribution during the preparation time in class (This has been monitored during in-class group work)

Part II: individual contribution to the biographical portion of the group project and its presentation (how well he/she is prepared to read from his/her research materials)

Part III: individual contributed to the presentation about hids/her selected story

Part IV: individual portion of the writing assignment was completed (analysis)

Part V: individual has provided all of his/her necessary portions of the group project (this includes the creation of a poster)

Name of Science Fiction Author: _______________________________

Student Name	Part I	Part II	Part III	Part IV	Part V	Total Score

LESSON FIFTEEN

<u>Objectives</u>
1. To review the main events and ideas in *The Time Machine*
2. To prepare students for the unit test

<u>Activity</u>
Choose one or more of the activities listed below and use your class time as directed.

REVIEW GAMES AND ACTIVITIES

1. Ask the class to make up a unit test for *The Time Machine.* The test should have 4 sections: matching, true/false, short answer, and essay. Students may use 1/2 of the class period to make the test and then swap papers and use the other 1/2 of the period to take a test a classmate has devised (open book). You may want to use the unit test included in this packet or take questions from the students' unit tests to formulate your own test.

2. Take 1/2 period for students to make up true and false questions (including the answers). Collect the papers and divide the class into two teams. Draw a big Tic-Tac-Toe board on the chalk board. Make one team X and one team O. Ask questions to each side, giving each student one turn. If the question is answered correctly, that student's team's letter (X or O) is placed in the box. If the answer is incorrect, no letter is placed in the box. The object is to get three in a row like Tic-Tac-Toe. You may want to keep track of the number of games won for each team.

3. Take 1/2 period for students to make up questions (true/false and short answer). Collect the questions. Divide the class into two teams. You'll alternate asking questions to individual members of teams A and B (like in a spelling bee). The question keeps going from A to B until it is correctly answered, then a new question is asked. A correct answer does not allow the team to get another question. Correct answers are +2 points; incorrect answers are -1 point.

4. Have students pair up and quiz each other from their study guides and class notes.

5. Give students a *The Time Machine* crossword puzzle to complete.

6. Divide your class into two teams. Use *The Time Machine* crossword words with their letters jumbled as a word list. Student 1 from Team A faces off against Student 1 from Team B. You write the first jumbled word on the board. The first student (1A or 1B) to unscramble the word wins the chance for his/her team to score points. If 1A wins the jumble, go to student 2A and give him/her a clue. He/she must give you the correct word which matches that clue. If he/she does, Team A scores a point, and you give student 3A a clue for which you expect another correct response. An incorrect response sends the game back to the jumbled-word face off, this time with students 2A and 2B. Instead of repeating giving clues to the first few students of each team, continue with the student after the one who gave the last incorrect response on the team. For examle, if Team B wins the jumbled-word face-off, and student 5B gave the last incorrect answer for Team B, you would start this round of clue questions with student 6B and so on. The team with the most points wins!

7. Play *What's My Line?*. This is similar to the old television show. Students assume the roles of different characters from the novel. One student gives clues to the class, or to a panel of contestants. The contestants try to guess the identity of the guest. Students may enjoy assisting you in creating rules and procedures for the game.

95

8. Play Jeopardy. Divide the class into two groups. Assign each group a category or chapter from the novel and have them devise answers for that category. Play the game according to the television show procedures.

9. Play *Drawing on the Details.* This is similar to *Pictionary.* Divide students into teams. A student from one team draws a scene from the novel. (You may want to specify the book or section.) Drawings should be kept simple, to keep the pace lively. Students in the opposing team locate the scene in their books and read it aloud. If they are incorrect, the illustrator's team has a chance to guess. Involve students in setting up a scoring system and any other necessary rules.

10. Play *I Have, Who Has?.* *NOTE This requires preparation in advance. On 3x5 cards, write a clue word on one side and a clue/definition question to another clue word on the other side of the card. Once you have completed a set, pass the cards out randomly, keeping one for yourself. You will start the game by saying, "Who has..." and reading the defintion/question on the card. The student who has the answer on his/her card that matches the definition/question shouts, "I have..." and reads the answer. He/she then turns over the card and says, "Who has..." and play continues until all the cards have been gone through.

11. Divide the class into two teams and play *Baseball.* The "pitcher" reads a question about the novel and in order to get a "hit" the "batter" must correctly answer the question. For this game, though, only one strike is allowed! If the "batter" gives the correct answer, he/she moves to the first base and the next "batter" comes up for another question. Score is kept like baseball with three outs and then the teams switch places.

LESSON SIXTEEN

<u>Objectives</u>
To test the students' understanding of the main ideas and themes in *The Time Machine*

<u>Activity #1</u>
Distribute the unit tests, give students ample time to complete them, and collect the tests when students finish. Remember to collect assigned books prior to the end of the class period.

NOTES ABOUT THE UNIT TESTS IN THIS UNIT:
There are 5 different unit tests included in the LitPlan Teacher Pack. Two are short answer, two are multiple choice. There is one advanced short answer test. The answers to the advanced short answer test will be based on the discussions you have had during class and should be graded accordingly. You should choose the tests and/or test parts which best suit your needs. Matching and short answer tests have answer keys. For essay type questions, grade according to your own criteria based on class discussions and the level of your students. Also, you will need to choose vocabulary words to read orally for the vocabulary section of the short answer tests.

<u>Activity #2</u>
Collect all test papers and assigned books prior to the end of the class period.

UNIT TESTS

The Time Machine SHORT ANSWER UNIT TEST 1

I. Matching/Identify

_____ 1.	ELOI	A.	Giant white statue in the forest
_____ 2.	NARRATOR	B.	The fourth dimension
_____ 3.	MEDICAL	C.	He was instructed to begin dinner promptly at 7:00 P.M.; the _______ Man
_____ 4.	CRAB	D.	He found himself on a very strange adventure; the Time _____.
_____ 5.	SPHINX	E.	He was the first to speak after the lengthy tale.
_____ 6.	FLOWERS	F.	Eloi believed that the Time Traveller came from this place.
_____ 7.	MATCHES	G.	People of the future had not seen these before.
_____ 8.	EDITOR	H.	The Eloi survived on this food.
_____ 9.	WEENA	I.	Morlocks feared it
_____ 10.	MORLOCKS	J.	Editor's name
_____ 11.	MEAT	K.	He seemed to be the most nervous person in the room; the _______ Man
_____ 12.	TRAVELLER	L.	She nearly drowned.
_____ 13.	MUSEUM	M.	He kept the Time Traveller's souvenir from the future.
_____ 14.	MACHINE	N.	The Time Traveller's souvenir from the future; wilted _______
_____ 15.	SILENT	O.	The Palace of Green Porcelain
_____ 16.	BLANK	P.	Industrious, underground carnivores
_____ 17.	FIRE	Q.	They had a peaceful, fruit-eating society.
_____ 18.	SUN	R.	It was hidden inside the bronze pedestal.
_____ 19.	FRUIT	S.	The Eloi were this to the Morlocks.
_____ 20.	TIME	T.	It attacked the Time Traveller in the far future; giant _______.

II. Short Answer

1. According to the Time Traveller, what four extensions must any real body have in order
   to exist?

2. How does the Time Traveller intend to prove his theory of time travel?

3. What does the Time Traveller show his guests after they witness his experiment?

4. The Time Traveller is late for the second dinner party. What is in the note he left for the
   Medical Man?

5. What is the condition of the Time Traveller when he enters the dining room?

6. What prohibits the Time Traveller from using his machine as he had planned?

7. What does the Time Traveller fear will happen if he stops the machine?

8. What does the Time Traveller do when the little people attempt to explore the machine?

9. How does the Time Traveller describe the little people who come to greet him?

10. Where does the Time Traveller think the inhabitants of the land believe he came from?

11. What does the Time Traveller discover when he returns to the area surrounding the White Sphinx on the first night?

12. When the Time Traveller goes to the second great hall trying to find the Time Machine, what does he use that the little people have forgotten?

13. What reaction does the Time Traveller receive when he suggests opening the doors to the bronze pedestal?

14. To what conclusion does the Time Traveller come regarding the creature he watched vanish down a deep shaft?

15.   What souvenir from the future world does the Time Traveller remove from his pocket to
      show his dinner guests?

16.   Why does the Time Traveller throw his shoes away?

17.   After finding a block of sulphur in one of the galleries, what does the Time Traveller
      think about making? Does he make it?

18.   What is the source of the "slumberous murmur" the Time Traveller hears in the forest?

19.   What does the Time Traveller see when he finally approaches the pedestal of the
      sphinx?"

20.   After escaping from the crab creatures, the Time Traveller goes thirty million years into
      the future. What does he see?

III. Essay

Explain how H. G. Wells' *The Time Machine* demonstrates at least three of the elements of science fiction as discussed in class.

IV. Vocabulary

Write the vocabulary words you are given. After writing them down, go back and
write in their definitions.

Word	Definition
1	
2	
3	
4	
5	
6	
7	
8	
9	
10	

I. Matching/Identify

Q	1.	ELOI	A.	Giant white statue in the forest
M	2.	NARRATOR	B.	The fourth dimension
C	3.	MEDICAL	C.	He was instructed to begin dinner promptly at 7:00 P.M.; the _______ Man
T	4.	CRAB	D.	He found himself on a very strange adventure; the Time _____.
A	5.	SPHINX	E.	He was the first to speak after the lengthy tale.
N	6.	FLOWERS	F.	Eloi believed that the Time Traveller came from this place.
G	7.	MATCHES	G.	People of the future had not seen these before.
E	8.	EDITOR	H.	The Eloi survived on this food.
L	9.	WEENA	I.	Morlocks feared it
P	10.	MORLOCKS	J.	Editor's name
S	11.	MEAT	K.	He seemed to be the most nervous person in the room; the _______ Man
D	12.	TRAVELLER	L.	She nearly drowned.
O	13.	MUSEUM	M.	He kept the Time Traveller's souvenir from the future.
R	14.	MACHINE	N.	The Time Traveller's souvenir from the future; wilted _______
K	15.	SILENT	O.	The Palace of Green Porcelain
J	16.	BLANK	P.	Industrious, underground carnivores
I	17.	FIRE	Q.	They had a peaceful, fruit-eating society.
F	18.	SUN	R.	It was hidden inside the bronze pedestal.
H	19.	FRUIT	S.	The Eloi were this to the Morlocks.
B	20.	TIME	T.	It attacked the Time Traveller in the far future; giant _______.

II. Short Answer

1. According to the Time Traveller, what four extensions must any real body have in order to exist?
   The Time Traveller claims that any real body must have length, breadth, thickness, and duration in order to exist.

2. How does the Time Traveller intend to prove his theory of time travel?
   The Time Traveller intends to prove his theory with the use of a small model of his Time Machine.

3. What does the Time Traveller show his guests after they witness his experiment?
   He shows the group a life-sized Time Machine intended for his use.

4. The Time Traveller is late for the second dinner party. What is in the note he left for the Medical Man?
   The note instructs the group to start dinner promptly at seven o'clock if he isn't there. It also says he will join them as soon as he can.

5. What is the condition of the Time Traveller when he enters the dining room?
   His coat is dusty, dirty, and smeared with green down the sleeves; his hair is disordered and greyer; his face is ghastly pale, and there is a half-healed cut on his chin.

6. What prohibits the Time Traveller from using his machine as he had planned?
   One of the nickel bars for the machine is too short and has to be fixed before the machine can be used.

7. What does the Time Traveller fear will happen if he stops the machine?
   He fears that if he stops the machine, he might blow up into the unknown.

8. What does the Time Traveller do when the little people attempt to explore the machine?
   To prevent them from accidentally setting the machine in motion, he unscrews the levers and puts them in his pocket.

9. How does the Time Traveller describe the little people who come to greet him?
   The little people have curly hair, but none on the face or neck; they have small ears, small mouths with bright, thin lips, pointed chins, and mild eyes.

10. Where does the Time Traveller think the inhabitants of the land believe he came from?
    He is certain the little people think he came from the sun in a thunderstorm.

11. What does the Time Traveller discover when he returns to the area surrounding the White Sphinx on the first night?
    He discovers the Time Machine is gone.

12. When the Time Traveller goes to the second great hall trying to find the Time Machine, what does he use that the little people have forgotten?
    He uses matches.

13. What reaction does the Time Traveller receive when he suggests opening the doors to the bronze pedestal?
    The little people become visibly upset.

14. To what conclusion does the Time Traveller come regarding the creature he watched vanish down a deep shaft?
    He believes there must be an underground society living in a great tunnel system beneath the world above.

15. What souvenir from the future world does the Time Traveller remove from his pocket to show his dinner guests?
    He removes two wilted flowers that Weena had given to him.

16. Why does the Time Traveller throw his shoes away?
    A nail from the heel of the shoe is pressing into his foot, and it causes his ankle to swell terribly.

17. After finding a block of sulphur in one of the galleries, what does the Time Traveller think about making? Does he make it?
He wonders if he could find the proper ingredients to make gunpowder. There is no saltpeter to be found, so he cannot make any gunpowder.

18. What is the source of the "slumberous murmur" the Time Traveller hears in the forest?
The fire the Time Traveller set earlier to scare the Morlocks has become a raging inferno burning the entire forest.

19. What does the Time Traveller see when he finally approaches the pedestal of the sphinx?"
He discovers the bronze doors to the pedestal are open.

20. After escaping from the crab creatures, the Time Traveller goes thirty million years into the future. What does he see?
The world is even darker than the world he just left. It is cold and snowy and absolutely silent. He sees no recognizable signs of life except for liverworts and lichen, and a football-sized creature with tentacles.

IV. Vocabulary

Write the vocabulary words and definitions you will use for this test.

Word	Definition
1	
2	
3	
4	
5	
6	
7	
8	
9	
10	

I. Matching/Identify

_____ 1.	ELOI	A.	The Time Traveller found this explosive in the museum
_____ 2.	NARRATOR	B.	They had a peaceful, fruit-eating society.
_____ 3.	MEDICAL	C.	He kept the Time Traveller's souvenir from the future.
_____ 4.	SPHINX	D.	He was instructed to begin dinner promptly at 7:00 P.M.; the _______ Man
_____ 5.	FLOWERS	E.	These have repositioned themselves over time.
_____ 6.	EDITOR	F.	Name of the Journalist
_____ 7.	WEENA	G.	She nearly drowned.
_____ 8.	MORLOCKS	H.	The very young man wanted to hear Greek from _____'s very lips.
_____ 9.	MUSEUM	I.	Eloi believed that the Time Traveller came from this place.
_____ 10.	SILENT	J.	The Time Traveller's souvenir from the future; wilted ______
_____ 11.	CHOSE	K.	The Time Traveller dreaded this.
_____ 12.	WATCHETT	L.	He was the first to speak after the lengthy tale.
_____ 13.	PLATO	M.	Silent Man's name
_____ 14.	DASH	N.	Giant white statue in the forest
_____ 15.	CAMPHOR	O.	The Eloi survived on this food.
_____ 16.	DYNAMITE	P.	Time Traveller's housekeeper
_____ 17.	SUN	Q.	Volatile substance the Time Traveller found in the museum
_____ 18.	FRUIT	R.	Industrious, underground carnivores
_____ 19.	DARKNESS	S.	The Palace of Green Porcelain
_____ 20.	STARS	T.	He seemed to be the most nervous person in the room; the _______ Man

II. Short Answer

1. What do the men see when the Psychologist presses the lever on the Time Machine model?

2. Who seems to become the most nervous when the Time Traveller sits down to dinner?

3. What does the Time Traveller notice when he tests the machine for the very first time?

4. What does the Time Traveller see when he stops the machine in the garden?

5. What does the Time Traveller notice about the little people and their society?

6. Although he is in great distress over the missing Time Machine, what one fact makes the Time Traveller feel assured?

7. What clues does the Time Traveller find that lead him to believe he knows the whereabouts of the time machine?

8.   How do the Time Traveller and Weena become friends?

9.   How does the Time Traveller describe the strange creature he encounters in a colossal ruin near the great hall?

10.   What does the Time Traveller learn about the diet of the Morlocks?

11.   What kind of meat does the Time Traveller believe he saw on the table in the Morlocks' cavern?

12.   What weapon does the Time Traveller believe would be the most effective against the Morlocks?

13.   What is the Palace of Green Porcelain?

14.   What does the Time Traveller find in one of the museum galleries that literally makes him dance?

15. What does the Time Traveller do that he later discovers to be an "atrocious folly?"

16. What does the Time Traveller notice about the Time Machine when he finds it?

17. How does the Time Traveller finally escape the Morlocks?

18. When the Time Traveller stops again, after escaping the Morlocks, what is the earth like?

19. What becomes of the Time Traveller?

20. What does the Narrator have as a reminder "that even when mind and strength had gone, gratitude and a mutual tenderness still lived in the heart of Man?"

III. Essay

Examine the Time Traveller's guest list. Why do you suppose he invites these specific men to witness his achievement? Why don't most of the men take the Time Traveller seriously? What does this say about their characters?

IV. Vocabulary

Write the vocabulary words you are given. After writing them down, go back and write in their definitions.

Word	Definition
1	
2	
3	
4	
5	
6	
7	
8	
9	
10	

I. Matching/Identify

B	1. ELOI	A.	The Time Traveller found this explosive in the museum
C	2. NARRATOR	B.	They had a peaceful, fruit-eating society.
D	3. MEDICAL	C.	He kept the Time Traveller's souvenir from the future.
N	4. SPHINX	D.	He was instructed to begin dinner promptly at 7:00 P.M.; the ______ Man
J	5. FLOWERS	E.	These have repositioned themselves over time.
L	6. EDITOR	F.	Name of the Journalist
G	7. WEENA	G.	She nearly drowned.
R	8. MORLOCKS	H.	The very young man wanted to hear Greek from ______'s very lips.
S	9. MUSEUM	I.	Eloi believed that the Time Traveller came from this place.
T	10. SILENT	J.	The Time Traveller's souvenir from the future; wilted ______
M	11. CHOSE	K.	The Time Traveller dreaded this.
P	12. WATCHETT	L.	He was the first to speak after the lengthy tale.
H	13. PLATO	M.	Silent Man's name
F	14. DASH	N.	Giant white statue in the forest
Q	15. CAMPHOR	O.	The Eloi survived on this food.
A	16. DYNAMITE	P.	Time Traveller's housekeeper
I	17. SUN	Q.	Volatile substance the Time Traveller found in the museum
O	18. FRUIT	R.	Industrious, underground carnivores
K	19. DARKNESS	S.	The Palace of Green Porcelain
E	20. STARS	T.	He seemed to be the most nervous person in the room; the ______ Man

II. Short Answer

1. What do the men see when the Psychologist presses the lever on the Time Machine model?
    When the Psychologist presses the lever on the Time Machine model, the machine disappears and no one knows where it is.

2. Who seems to become the most nervous when the Time Traveller sits down to dinner?
    The Silent Man seems to be the most nervous.

3. What does the Time Traveller notice when he tests the machine for the very first time?
    He notices the clock in his laboratory goes from 10:01 to 3:20 in a matter of seconds.

4. What does the Time Traveller see when he stops the machine in the garden?
    He sees a lawn surrounded by rhododendron bushes and a colossal white marble figure in the shape of a winged sphinx.

5. What does the Time Traveller notice about the little people and their society?
    He notices that no one seems to do work of any kind, and they do not live in separate houses, but in sort of communal buildings. He also notes they eat only fruits and absolutely no meat. He feels as if he is in some kind of utopia.

6. Although he is in great distress over the missing Time Machine, what one fact makes the Time Traveller feel assured?
    The Time Machine could not have been moved in time because he has the levers in his pocket. It has to have been moved to a different location in the present time.

7. What clues does the Time Traveller find that lead him to believe he knows the whereabouts of the time machine?
    He finds a groove and a series of footprints on the ground leading to the bronze pedestal of the statue.

8. How do the Time Traveller and Weena become friends?
    The Time Traveller saves her from drowning in the river.

9. How does the Time Traveller describe the strange creature he encounters in a colossal ruin near the great hall?
    The creature is a dull white, ape-like creature with large grayish-red eyes. It has flaxen hair on its head and down its back.

10. What does the Time Traveller learn about the diet of the Morlocks?
    He learns the Morlocks are meat eaters.

11. What kind of meat does the Time Traveller believe he saw on the table in the Morlocks' cavern?
    The Time Traveller is certain that the pieces of meat he'd seen on the table were captured Eloi (upper world people).

12. What weapon does the Time Traveller believe would be the most effective against the Morlocks?
    He believes fire would be the best weapon against the Morlocks.

13. What is the Palace of Green Porcelain?
    The Palace of Green Porcelain is a museum.

14. What does the Time Traveller find in one of the museum galleries that literally makes him dance?
    He finds a box of matches that are still good.

15. What does the Time Traveller do that he later discovers to be an "atrocious folly?"
    He lights the firewood to cover his retreat from the Morlocks.

16. What does the Time Traveller notice about the Time Machine when he finds it?
    He discovers that the Morlocks have oiled and cleaned the machine thoroughly.

17. How does the Time Traveller finally escape the Morlocks?
    He fights the Morlocks while he inserts the levers. He is finally able to operate the time machine and disappear.

18. When the Time Traveller stops again, after escaping the Morlocks, what is the earth like?
    It's a very dark, dismal place because the earth no longer turns on its axis. The Time Traveller has landed on the dark side of the planet.

19. What becomes of the Time Traveller?
    The Narrator sees him in the Time Machine, and then he vanishes. The Time Traveller never returns.

20. What does the Narrator have as a reminder "that even when mind and strength had gone, gratitude and a mutual tenderness still lived in the heart of Man?"
    The Narrator keeps the two wilted flowers Weena had given the Time Traveller.

IV. Vocabulary
Write the vocabulary words and definitions you will use for this test.

Word	Definition
1	
2	
3	
4	
5	
6	
7	
8	
9	
10	

The Time Machine ADVANCED SHORT ANSWER TEST

I. Matching/Identify

____ 1.	ELOI	A.	Silent Man's name
____ 2.	NARRATOR	B.	Morlocks feared it
____ 3.	MEDICAL	C.	Publisher the Time Traveller never got to meet with
____ 4.	FLOWERS	D.	The Time Traveller's souvenir from the future; wilted ______
____ 5.	WEENA	E.	Argumentative person with red hair
____ 6.	MORLOCKS	F.	Industrious, underground carnivores
____ 7.	RICHARDSON	G.	The Time Traveller found this explosive in the museum
____ 8.	CHOSE	H.	The fourth dimension
____ 9.	WATCHETT	I.	She nearly drowned.
____ 10.	PLATO	J.	Editor's name
____ 11.	BLANK	K.	This was a clue as to where the time machine was hidden.
____ 12.	DASH	L.	The Eloi survived on this food.
____ 13.	FILBY	M.	They had a peaceful, fruit-eating society.
____ 14.	FIRE	N.	These have repositioned themselves over time.
____ 15.	CAMPHOR	O.	The very young man wanted to hear Greek from ______'s very lips.
____ 16.	DYNAMITE	P.	He kept the Time Traveller's souvenir from the future.
____ 17.	FRUIT	Q.	Name of the Journalist
____ 18.	GROOVE	R.	Time Traveller's housekeeper
____ 19.	TIME	S.	He was instructed to begin dinner promptly at 7:00 P.M.; the ______ Man
____ 20.	STARS	T.	Volatile substance the Time Traveller found in the museum

II. Short Answer

1. Discuss three specific character traits for the Time Traveller. Cite evidence from the text that shows these traits.

2. What elements of setting are important to the science fiction novel? Why?

3. Explain what caused the Morlocks to seek refuge beneath the ground. While underground, they maintain the technical aspects (machines, production of goods) that the present society views as "civilized," yet the Time Traveller is horrified by them. What horrifies him? What might H. G. Wells be saying about present society?

4. Explain the symbolism of the wilted flowers. What do they mean to the Time Traveller? What do they mean to the Narrator?

5. H. G. Wells paints a bleak picture of the future of the earth and civilization. Why might he depict such a terrible projection? What might Wells be saying about tendencies in the behavior of the human race?

6. How does the seemingly Utopian society of the Eloi act as a source of irony in the novel? How about the Morlocks' caves?

III. Essay

Thinking back over the classroom presentations about authors in the science fiction genre, select two different authors and show how each wrote stories that exhibited elements of sci-fi as discussed in class.

IV. Vocabulary
   A. Write the vocabulary words you are given. After writing them down, go back and
      write in their definitions.

Word	Definition
1	
2	
3	
4	
5	
6	
7	
8	
9	
10	

   B. Write a paragraph about the book using 8 of the 10 vocabulary words above.

I. Matching/Identify

M	1.	ELOI	A.	Silent Man's name
P	2.	NARRATOR	B.	Morlocks feared it
S	3.	MEDICAL	C.	Publisher the Time Traveller never got to meet with
D	4.	FLOWERS	D.	The Time Traveller's souvenir from the future; wilted _______
I	5.	WEENA	E.	Argumentative person with red hair
F	6.	MORLOCKS	F.	Industrious, underground carnivores
C	7.	RICHARDSON	G.	The Time Traveller found this explosive in the museum
A	8.	CHOSE	H.	The fourth dimension
R	9.	WATCHETT	I.	She nearly drowned.
O	10.	PLATO	J.	Editor's name
J	11.	BLANK	K.	This was a clue as to where the time machine was hidden.
Q	12.	DASH	L.	The Eloi survived on this food.
E	13.	FILBY	M.	They had a peaceful, fruit-eating society.
B	14.	FIRE	N.	These have repositioned themselves over time.
T	15.	CAMPHOR	O.	The very young man wanted to hear Greek from _______'s very lips.
G	16.	DYNAMITE	P.	He kept the Time Traveller's souvenir from the future.
L	17.	FRUIT	Q.	Name of the Journalist
K	18.	GROOVE	R.	Time Traveller's housekeeper
H	19.	TIME	S.	He was instructed to begin dinner promptly at 7:00 P.M.; the _______ Man
N	20.	STARS	T.	Volatile substance the Time Traveller found in the museum

IV. Vocabulary
     Write the vocabulary words and definitions you will use for this test.

Word	Definition
1	
2	
3	
4	
5	
6	
7	
8	
9	
10	

The Time Machine MULTIPLE CHOICE UNIT TEST 1

I. Matching/Identify

____ 1.	ELOI	A.	Industrious, underground carnivores
____ 2.	NARRATOR	B.	Volatile substance the Time Traveller found in the museum
____ 3.	MEDICAL	C.	Name of the Journalist
____ 4.	CRAB	D.	He was the first to speak after the lengthy tale.
____ 5.	SPHINX	E.	He seemed to be the most nervous person in the room; the ______ Man
____ 6.	FLOWERS	F.	Giant white statue in the forest
____ 7.	MATCHES	G.	The Time Traveller's souvenir from the future; wilted ______
____ 8.	EDITOR	H.	The Palace of Green Porcelain
____ 9.	WEENA	I.	It was hidden inside the bronze pedestal.
____ 10.	MORLOCKS	J.	People of the future had not seen these before.
____ 11.	MEAT	K.	She nearly drowned.
____ 12.	TRAVELLER	L.	He found himself on a very strange adventure; the Time ______.
____ 13.	MUSEUM	M.	Time Traveller's housekeeper
____ 14.	MACHINE	N.	He was instructed to begin dinner promptly at 7:00 P.M.; the ______ Man
____ 15.	SILENT	O.	They had a peaceful, fruit-eating society.
____ 16.	CHOSE	P.	The Eloi were this to the Morlocks.
____ 17.	WATCHETT	Q.	It attacked the Time Traveller in the far future; giant ______.
____ 18.	DASH	R.	He kept the Time Traveller's souvenir from the future.
____ 19.	CAMPHOR	S.	The Time Traveller found this explosive in the museum
____ 20.	DYNAMITE	T.	Silent Man's name

II. Multiple Choice

1. According to the Time Traveller, what four extensions must any real body have in order to exist?
    A. Length, breadth, thickness, and duration
    B. Height, width, volume, and velocity
    C. Length, breadth, thickness, and weight
    D. Light, sound, weight, and opaqueness

2. How does the Time Traveller intend to prove his theory of time travel?
    A. He has created a small model of his Time Machine to show the men how it works.
    B. He is going to synchronize his watch with the gentlemen's watches and then travel ten minutes into the future.
    C. He plans to send the Psychologist ten minutes into the future.
    D. He intends to bring items from the past into the present.

3. What does the Time Traveller show his guests after they witness his experiment?
    A. He shows them his watch, which is precisely ten minutes behind the time on their own watches.
    B. He show them the plans for a life-sized model of the Time Machine.
    C. The Psychologist's watch is one minute behind his own watch.
    D. He shows them a life-sized Time Machine he built for his own use.

4. The Time Traveller is late for the second dinner party. What is in the note he left for the Medical Man?
    A. The Time Traveller instructs the Medical Man to meet him at his laboratory at precisely 6:48 P.M.
    B. The Time Traveller instructs the Medical Man to contact the police if he is more than one hour late for dinner.
    C. The Time Traveller instructs the Medical Man to begin dinner promptly at 7:00.
    D. The Time Traveller instructs the Medical Man to use the time machine to join him in the future.

5. What is the condition of the Time Traveller when he enters the dining room?
    A. He is dressed for dinner but looks very tired and has lost weight.
    B. His hair is greyer, and he has a half-healed cut on his face. His clothes are dusty and dirty.
    C. He is feverish, collapses into the room, and becomes unconscious.
    D. He is dressed in a smoking jacket, is carrying a pipe, and is smoking triumphantly.

6. What prohibits the Time Traveller from using his machine as he had planned?
    A. He discovers the machine does not work, and he has to rebuild it.
    B. One of the nickel bars is too short and has to be replaced.
    C. He is suffering from a terrible fever that has lasted for five days.
    D. He is afraid to use the machine because he doesn't know if he will survive the trip.

7. What does the Time Traveller fear will happen if he stops the machine?
    A. He is afraid he will never return to his own time period.
    B. He is afraid the machine will not stop at all.
    C. He is afraid he will not be able to find the fuel needed to run the machine.
    D. He is afraid he will blow up into the unknown.

8. What does the Time Traveller do when the little people attempt to explore the machine?
    A. He unscrews the levers that make the machine work and puts them in his pocket.
    B. He gets back in the machine and leaves.
    C. He yells and waves them away from the machine.
    D. He distracts their attention by walking away from the machine.

9. How does the Time Traveller describe the little people who come to greet him?
    A. They are small with long straight hair, pale lips, and wild eyes.
    B. They are extremely tall and bronze with superhuman strength.
    C. They are small with curly hair, bright lips, pointed chins, and mild eyes.
    D. They are pale-complexioned with flaxen hair and greyish-red eyes.

10. Where does the Time Traveller think the inhabitants of the land believe he came from?
    A. They believe he came from the sun during a thunderstorm.
    B. They believe he came from below ground.
    C. They believe he came from the other side of the planet.
    D. They believe he came from the moon.

11. What does the Time Traveller discover when he returns to the area surrounding the White Sphinx on the first night?
    A. Someone has smashed the dials of the Time Machine.
    B. He discovers the Time Machine is gone.
    C. He finds a young boy examining the Time Machine closely.
    D. The statue of the White Sphinx has been beheaded.

12.   When the Time Traveller goes to the second great hall trying to find the Time Machine, what item does he use that the little people have forgotten?

A. Scissors

B. Matches

C. Eye glasses

D. Magnifying glasses

13.   What reaction does the Time Traveller receive when he suggests opening the doors to the bronze pedestel?

A. The little people become visibly upset.

B. The little people begin banging on the doors.

C. The little people ignore him and go about their business.

D. The little people become very happy.

14.   To what conclusion does the Time Traveller come regarding the creature he watched vanish down a deep shaft?

A. The creature must belong to some underground society that lives in tunnels below.

B. He realizes that spiders have evolved and now live underground.

C. The giant creature is strong enough to carry the Time Machine away.

D. The serpent is what caused the little people so much fear.

15.   What souvenir from the future world does the Time Traveller remove from his pocket to show his dinner guests?

A. A necklace made by Weena

B. A lump of camphor

C. A box of matches

D. Two wilted flowers

16.   Why does the Time Traveller throw his shoes away?

A. The shoes leave specific footprints for the Morlocks to follow.

B. A nail keeps poking him in the heel, and his ankle has become swollen.

C. He no longer needs them.

D. He tries to blend in with the Eloi, so he discards all his clothing from his own time.

17.   After finding a block of sulphur in one of the galleries, what idea sets the Time Traveller's mind racing?
    A. He can use all the blocks he's found to create a stronghold for himself.
    B. He can place the lighted sulphur blocks at the openings of the Morlocks' caves to keep them in at night.
    C. He believes the terrible smell of sulphur burning will keep the Morlocks away.
    D. He wonders if he can find the proper ingredients to make gunpowder.

18.   What is the source of the "slumberous murmur" the Time Traveller hears in the forest?
    A. It is the sound of the Time Traveller snoring.
    B. It is the sound of a forest fire roaring.
    C. It is the sound the Eloi make trying to scare the Morlocks.
    D. It is the sound of the only creature the Morlocks fear.

19.   What does the Time Traveller see when he finally approaches the pedestal of the sphinx?
    A. The broken stone head of the sphinx is actually the key to get inside the pedestal.
    B. The doors of the pedestal are standing open.
    C. The time machine is standing outside the pedestal.
    D. The Eloi have boarded up the entrance to the pedestal.

20.   After escaping from the crab creatures the Time Traveller goes thiry million years into the future. What does he see?
    A. The world is a lush garden paradise.
    B. The world is a dark, mountainous region ruled by primitive humans.
    C. The world is cold, snowy, and absolutely silent.
    D. It is merely an empty space; the earth has been destroyed.

III. Composition
1. What is the main conflict in H. G. Wells's *The Time Machine*? Fully describe the
    conflict and how it is (or is not) resolved.

2. How does the fact that a portion of the novel is set in 19th Century England play an
    important part in the events of the plot? What elements of life in the 19th Century seem
    to play a key role?

3. H. G. Wells paints a bleak picture of the future of the earth and civilization. Why might he depict such a terrible projection? What might Wells be saying about tendencies in the behavior of the human race?

4. Weena is the only Eloi given a name in the novel. How does the fact that the Time Traveller names her set her apart from the rest of society? How does the fact that she has a name make her death all the more tragic?

IV. Vocabulary

____ 1.	VELOCITY	A.	The meat of sheep
____ 2.	IMPARTIALITY	B.	Reckless boldness; rashness
____ 3.	MUTTON	C.	Ghostly
____ 4.	POIGNANT	D.	Lacking the ability to express oneself, esp. in clear speech
____ 5.	TEMERITY	E.	Dirty
____ 6.	DILAPIDATED	F.	Small brook; rivulet
____ 7.	INDOLENT	G.	Given or received in return for services, debt, injury, lack, etc.
____ 8.	INARTICULATE	H.	Fallen into partial ruin or decay, as from age, wear, or neglect
____ 9.	TETHERED	I.	Lizards or similar reptiles
____ 10.	PALLID	J.	Rapidity of motion or operation; swiftness; speed
____ 11.	SPECTRAL	K.	Pale; faint or deficient in color
____ 12.	IMPEDED	L.	Showing a disposition to avoid exertion; slothful; lazy
____ 13.	RILL	M.	Relating to algae
____ 14.	RECEDED	N.	Showing no bias; neutrality
____ 15.	SUCCULENT	O.	Moved away; retreated; withdrew
____ 16.	COMPENSATION	P.	Confined or restricted with or as if with a rope or chain
____ 17.	TUMULT	Q.	Highly distressing agitation of mind or feeling
____ 18.	ALGAL	R.	Affecting or moving the emotions
____ 19.	BEGRIMED	S.	Slowed or obstructed the progress of
____ 20.	SAURIANS	T.	Full of juice; juicy

I. Matching/Identify

O	1. ELOI	A.	Industrious, underground carnivores
R	2. NARRATOR	B.	Volatile substance the Time Traveller found in the museum
N	3. MEDICAL	C.	Name of the Journalist
Q	4. CRAB	D.	He was the first to speak after the lengthy tale.
F	5. SPHINX	E.	He seemed to be the most nervous person in the room; the _______ Man
G	6. FLOWERS	F.	Giant white statue in the forest
J	7. MATCHES	G.	The Time Traveller's souvenir from the future; wilted _______
D	8. EDITOR	H.	The Palace of Green Porcelain
K	9. WEENA	I.	It was hidden inside the bronze pedestal.
A	10. MORLOCKS	J.	People of the future had not seen these before.
P	11. MEAT	K.	She nearly drowned.
L	12. TRAVELLER	L.	He found himself on a very strange adventure; the Time _______.
H	13. MUSEUM	M.	Time Traveller's housekeeper
I	14. MACHINE	N.	He was instructed to begin dinner promptly at 7:00 P.M.; the _______ Man
E	15. SILENT	O.	They had a peaceful, fruit-eating society.
T	16. CHOSE	P.	The Eloi were this to the Morlocks.
M	17. WATCHETT	Q.	It attacked the Time Traveller in the far future; giant _______.
C	18. DASH	R.	He kept the Time Traveller's souvenir from the future.
B	19. CAMPHOR	S.	The Time Traveller found this explosive in the museum
S	20. DYNAMITE	T.	Silent Man's name

II. Multiple Choice

A 1.   According to the Time Traveller, what four extensions must any real body have in order to exist?

    A.   Length, breadth, thickness, and duration

    B.   Height, width, volume, and velocity

    C.   Length, breadth, thickness, and weight

    D.   Light, sound, weight, and opaqueness

A 2.   How does the Time Traveller intend to prove his theory of time travel?

    A.   He has created a small model of his Time Machine to show the men how it works.

    B.   He is going to synchronize his watch with the gentlemen's watches and then travel ten minutes into the future.

    C.   He plans to send the Psychologist ten minutes into the future.

    D.   He intends to bring items from the past into the present.

D 3.   What does the Time Traveller show his guests after they witness his experiment?

    A.   He shows them his watch, which is precisely ten minutes behind the time on their own watches.

    B.   He show them the plans for a life-sized model of the Time Machine.

    C.   The Psychologist's watch is one minute behind his own watch.

    D.   He shows them a life-sized Time Machine he built for his own use.

C 4.   The Time Traveller is late for the second dinner party. What is in the note he left for the Medical Man?

    A.   The Time Traveller instructs the Medical Man to meet him at his laboratory at precisely 6:48 P.M.

    B.   The Time Traveller instructs the Medical Man to contact the police if he is more than one hour late for dinner.

    C.   The Time Traveller instructs the Medical Man to begin dinner promptly at 7:00.

    D.   The Time Traveller instructs the Medical Man to use the time machine to join him in the future.

B 5.   What is the condition of the Time Traveller when he enters the dining room?

    A.   He is dressed for dinner but looks very tired and has lost weight.

    B.   His hair is greyer, and he has a half-healed cut on his face. His clothes are dusty and dirty.

    C.   He is feverish, collapses into the room, and becomes unconscious.

    D.   He is dressed in a smoking jacket, is carrying a pipe, and is smoking triumphantly.

B 6.   What prohibits the Time Traveller from using his machine as he had planned?
   A. He discovers the machine does not work, and he has to rebuild it.
   B. One of the nickel bars is too short and has to be replaced.
   C. He is suffering from a terrible fever that has lasted for five days.
   D. He is afraid to use the machine because he doesn't know if he will survive the trip.

D 7.   What does the Time Traveller fear will happen if he stops the machine?
   A. He is afraid he will never return to his own time period.
   B. He is afraid the machine will not stop at all.
   C. He is afraid he will not be able to find the fuel needed to run the machine.
   D. He is afraid he will blow up into the unknown.

A 8.   What does the Time Traveller do when the little people attempt to explore the machine?
   A. He unscrews the levers that make the machine work and puts them in his pocket.
   B. He gets back in the machine and leaves.
   C. He yells and waves them away from the machine.
   D. He distracts their attention by walking away from the machine.

C 9.   How does the Time Traveller describe the little people who come to greet him?
   A. They are small with long straight hair, pale lips, and wild eyes.
   B. They are extremely tall and bronze with superhuman strength.
   C. They are small with curly hair, bright lips, pointed chins, and mild eyes.
   D. They are pale-complexioned with flaxen hair and greyish-red eyes.

A 10.   Where does the Time Traveller think the inhabitants of the land believe he came from?
   A. They believe he came from the sun during a thunderstorm.
   B. They believe he came from below ground.
   C. They believe he came from the other side of the planet.
   D. They believe he came from the moon.

B 11.   What does the Time Traveller discover when he returns to the area surrounding the
White Sphinx on the first night?
   A. Someone has smashed the dials of the Time Machine.
   B. He discovers the Time Machine is gone.
   C. He finds a young boy examining the Time Machine closely.
   D. The statue of the White Sphinx has been beheaded.

B 12.   When the Time Traveller goes to the second great hall trying to find the Time Machine,
what item does he use that the little people have forgotten?

    A.   Scissors

    B.   Matches

    C.   Eye glasses

    D.   Magnifying glasses

A 13.   What reaction does the Time Traveller receive when he suggests opening the doors to
the bronze pedestel?

    A.   The little people become visibly upset.

    B.   The little people begin banging on the doors.

    C.   The little people ignore him and go about their business.

    D.   The little people become very happy.

A 14.   To what conclusion does the Time Traveller come regarding the creature he watched
vanish down a deep shaft?

    A.   The creature must belong to some underground society that lives in tunnels below.

    B.   He realizes that spiders have evolved and now live underground.

    C.   The giant creature is strong enough to carry the Time Machine away.

    D.   The serpent is what caused the little people so much fear.

D 15.   What souvenir from the future world does the Time Traveller remove from his pocket to
show his dinner guests?

    A.   A necklace made by Weena

    B.   A lump of camphor

    C.   A box of matches

    D.   Two wilted flowers

B 16.   Why does the Time Traveller throw his shoes away?

    A.   The shoes leave specific footprints for the Morlocks to follow.

    B.   A nail keeps poking him in the heel, and his ankle has become swollen.

    C.   He no longer needs them.

    D.   He tries to blend in with the Eloi, so he discards all his clothing from his own time.

D 17. After finding a block of sulphur in one of the galleries, what idea sets the Time
Traveller's mind racing?

    A. He can use all the blocks he's found to create a stronghold for himself.

    B. He can place the lighted sulphur blocks at the openings of the Morlocks' caves to
keep them in at night.

    C. He believes the terrible smell of sulphur burning will keep the Morlocks away.

    D. He wonders if he can find the proper ingredients to make gunpowder.

B 18. What is the source of the "slumberous murmur" the Time Traveller hears in the forest?

    A. It is the sound of the Time Traveller snoring.

    B. It is the sound of a forest fire roaring.

    C. It is the sound the Eloi make trying to scare the Morlocks.

    D. It is the sound of the only creature the Morlocks fear.

B 19. What does the Time Traveller see when he finally approaches the pedestal of the sphinx?

    A. The broken stone head of the sphinx is actually the key to get inside the pedestal.

    B. The doors of the pedestal are standing open.

    C. The time machine is standing outside the pedestal.

    D. The Eloi have boarded up the entrance to the pedestal.

C 20. After escaping from the crab creatures the Time Traveller goes thiry million years into
the future. What does he see?

    A. The world is a lush garden paradise.

    B. The world is a dark, mountainous region ruled by primitive humans.

    C. The world is cold, snowy, and absolutely silent.

    D. It is merely an empty space; the earth has been destroyed.

IV. Vocabulary

J	1.	VELOCITY	A.	The meat of sheep
N	2.	IMPARTIALITY	B.	Reckless boldness; rashness
A	3.	MUTTON	C.	Ghostly
R	4.	POIGNANT	D.	Lacking the ability to express oneself, esp. in clear speech
B	5.	TEMERITY	E.	Dirty
H	6.	DILAPIDATED	F.	Small brook; rivulet
L	7.	INDOLENT	G.	Given or received in return for services, debt, injury, lack, etc.
D	8.	INARTICULATE	H.	Fallen into partial ruin or decay, as from age, wear, or neglect
P	9.	TETHERED	I.	Lizards or similar reptiles
K	10.	PALLID	J.	Rapidity of motion or operation; swiftness; speed
C	11.	SPECTRAL	K.	Pale; faint or deficient in color
S	12.	IMPEDED	L.	Showing a disposition to avoid exertion; slothful; lazy
F	13.	RILL	M.	Relating to algae
O	14.	RECEDED	N.	Showing no bias; neutrality
T	15.	SUCCULENT	O.	Moved away; retreated; withdrew
G	16.	COMPENSATION	P.	Confined or restricted with or as if with a rope or chain
Q	17.	TUMULT	Q.	Highly distressing agitation of mind or feeling
M	18.	ALGAL	R.	Affecting or moving the emotions
E	19.	BEGRIMED	S.	Slowed or obstructed the progress of
I	20.	SAURIANS	T.	Full of juice; juicy

I. Matching/Identify

____ 1.	ELOI	A.	The Eloi were this to the Morlocks.
____ 2.	NARRATOR	B.	The very young man wanted to hear Greek from ______'s very lips.
____ 3.	MEDICAL	C.	She nearly drowned.
____ 4.	CRAB	D.	Giant white statue in the forest
____ 5.	SPHINX	E.	The Time Traveller's souvenir from the future; wilted ______
____ 6.	FLOWERS	F.	He kept the Time Traveller's souvenir from the future.
____ 7.	MATCHES	G.	Morlocks used this when cleaning the time machine.
____ 8.	EDITOR	H.	He found himself on a very strange adventure; the Time ______.
____ 9.	WEENA	I.	They had a peaceful, fruit-eating society.
____ 10.	MORLOCKS	J.	It attacked the Time Traveller in the far future; giant ______.
____ 11.	MEAT	K.	He seemed to be the most nervous person in the room; the ______ Man
____ 12.	TRAVELLER	L.	The Time Traveller found this explosive in the museum
____ 13.	MUSEUM	M.	It was hidden inside the bronze pedestal.
____ 14.	MACHINE	N.	The Eloi survived on this food.
____ 15.	SILENT	O.	He was the first to speak after the lengthy tale.
____ 16.	PLATO	P.	He was instructed to begin dinner promptly at 7:00 P.M.; the ______ Man
____ 17.	DYNAMITE	Q.	Industrious, underground carnivores
____ 18.	OIL	R.	People of the future had not seen these before.
____ 19.	FRUIT	S.	The Palace of Green Porcelain
____ 20.	TIME	T.	The fourth dimension

1. What do the men see when the Psychologist presses the lever on the Time Machine model?
    A. Nothing happens.
    B. The model disappears before their eyes.
    C. The Time Machine explodes in a cloud of smoke.
    D. The Psychologist disappears before their eyes.

2. Who seems to become the most nervous when the Time Traveller sits down to dinner?
    A. The Medical Man
    B. The Silent Man
    C. The Psychologist
    D. The Narrator

3. What does the Time Traveller notice when he uses the machine for the very first time?
    A. The crystal needed to activate the machine is cracked.
    B. He feels like he is sleep walking.
    C. Nothing happens when he tries the machine the first time.
    D. The time on the clock goes from 10:01 to 3:30.

4. What does the Time Traveller see when he stops the machine in the garden?
    A. He sees a lawn surrounded by rhododendron bushes and a colossal white marble figure in the shape of a winged sphinx.
    B. He sees the moon and realizes it is too close to the earth.
    C. He sees a huge castle made of glass.
    D. He sees a small village in the distance, but no people.

5. What does the Time Traveller notice about the little people and their society?
    A. Both the men and the women are fierce hunters and warriors.
    B. No one seems to do any work. They eat fruit all day and sleep in communal houses.
    C. The people have superhuman intelligence and are able to move things with their minds.
    D. They are a contemplative society that spends days discussing philosophical issues.

6. Although he is in great distress over the missing Time Machine, what one fact makes the Time Traveller feel reassured?

    A. He has the levers to work the machine in his pocket.

    B. He knew even if he could not get home, he would be very happy living with the little people.

    C. He has the key to start the machine in his pocket.

    D. He has the plans to the machine in his pocket and can build a new machine.

7. What clue does the Time Traveller find that leads him to believe he knows the whereabouts of the Time Machine?

    A. There are grooves and footprints in the dirt in front of the bronze pedestal.

    B. He overhears a group of the people talking; they mention a cave in the forest.

    C. There is a trail of broken parts leading into the forest.

    D. There is a note in his pocket telling him the machine has been "borrowed."

8. How do the Time Traveller and Weena become friends?

    A. He asks her to serve as a guide into the wilderness as he looks for his Time Machine.

    B. Weena's father gives her to the Time Traveller as a gift.

    C. Weena feels pity for him because he is alone, so she hangs out with him.

    D. The Time Traveller saves her from drowning.

9. How does the Time Traveller describe the strange creature he encounters in a colossal ruin near the great hall?

    A. He sees a dull white, ape-like creature with grayish-red eyes.

    B. He sees a seven-foot man-like creature covered with fur.

    C. He sees a great serpent with bright yellow eyes and huge fangs.

    D. He sees a huge spider-like creature with large claws, long antennae, and many legs.

10. What does the Time Traveller learn about the diet of the Morlocks?

    A. They are vegetarians.

    B. They only eat once a week.

    C. They are carnivores.

    D. They eat the rodents that live in their caves.

11.   What is the "clear knowledge" regarding the meat seen by the Time Traveller in the Morlocks' caverns?

   A.   The meat on the white table is an Eloi; the Morlocks eat them.

   B.   The Morlocks are cannibals; they eat each other.

   C.   The Morlocks use the meat to try to capture the giant serpent that lives underground.

   D.   The meat is placed there as bait to draw the Time Traveller into the caverns.

12.   What weapon does the Time Traveller believe would be the most effective against the Morlocks?

   A.   Fire

   B.   A mace

   C.   A crossbow

   D.   Dynamite

13.   What is the Palace of Green Porcelain?

   A.   It is the Time Traveller's own house.

   B.   It is an ancient museum.

   C.   It is an ancient bank.

   D.   It is an ancient train station.

14.   What does the Time Traveller find in one of the galleries that literally makes him dance?

   A.   He finds books that he himself had published about time travel.

   B.   He finds canned foods that were still good enough to eat.

   C.   He finds two workable sticks of dynamite.

   D.   He finds a box of matches.

15.   What does the Time Traveller do that he later discovers to be an "atrocious folly?"

   A.   He runs into the woods without first checking his whereabouts.

   B.   He leaves Weena unguarded near a hollow tree.

   C.   He throws the sticks of dynamite at the Morlocks.

   D.   He lights the firewood to frighten the Morlocks.

16.   What does the Time Traveller notice about the Time Machine when he finds it?

   A.   The dials are broken; he doesn't know if the machine will work.

   B.   The Morlocks have cleaned and oiled it thoroughly.

   C.   It is covered with a slimy film from being underground.

   D.   The crystal that makes it work is now cracked.

17. How does the Time Traveller finally escape the Morlocks?
    A. The Eloi come to his rescue and distract the Morlocks long enough for him to leave.
    B. He throws a stick of dynamite at them and blows them up.
    C. He lures them to a tunnel he has filled with gunpowder. He then sets off the charge, sealing the Morlocks inside.
    D. He fights the Morlocks while he inserts the levers into the machine. He is able to turn it on and escape.

18. When the Time Traveller stops again after escaping the Morlocks, what is the earth like?
    A. It is more beautiful than the Time Traveller remembered.
    B. It is cold and very dark.
    C. It is a very dark, dismal place.
    D. It is covered in water.

19. What becomes of the Time Traveller?
    A. He is so traumatized by his experiences that he destroys the time machine.
    B. He enters the time machine once more and is never seen again.
    C. He becomes world-famous for his invention.
    D. He is committed to an insane asylum.

20. What does the Narrator have as a reminder "that even when mind and strength had gone, gratitude and a mutual tenderness still lived in the heart of Man?"
    A. The Narrator has become closer friends with the Time Traveller.
    B. The Narrator has the two wilted flowers.
    C. The Narrator has the miniature model of the time machine.
    D. The Narrator has the Time Traveller's journal of his adventures.

1. Discuss three specific character traits for the Time Traveller. Cite examples of these tratits from the text.

2. Examine the Time Traveller's guest list. Why do you suppose he invites these specific men to witness his achievement? Why don't most of the men take the Time Traveller seriously? What does this say about their characters?

3. The Narrator seems to be the only man who believes the Time Traveller. What convinces him? Why does he keep the flowers from the Time Traveller's pocket? What do these actions say about the character of the Narrator?

4. How does the seemingly Utopian society of the Eloi act as a source of irony in the novel? How about the Morlocks' caves?

IV. Vocabulary

_____ 1.	INCREDULOUS	A.	In a condition or process of mental or moral decay
_____ 2.	JOCULAR	B.	Avoid or escape by speed, cleverness, or trickery; to evade
_____ 3.	ANECDOTES	C.	Short accounts of interesting or humorous incidents
_____ 4.	COLOSSAL	D.	Showing a disposition to avoid exertion; slothful; lazy
_____ 5.	FRUGIVOROUS	E.	Out of the ordinary course of nature; exceptionally or abnormally
_____ 6.	INDOLENT	F.	Feeding on fruit; fruit eating
_____ 7.	PRECOCIOUS	G.	A club-like armor-breaking weapon of war
_____ 8.	INTIMATE	H.	Brilliantly or excessively showy
_____ 9.	DECADENT	I.	Great misfortune or disaster
_____ 10.	INTERMINABLE	J.	Compound used in the manufacture of plastics and explosives
_____ 11.	PRETERNATURALLY	K.	To indicate or make known indirectly; hint; imply; suggest
_____ 12.	MACE	L.	Creation of the imagination or fancy; fantasy
_____ 13.	CAMPHOR	M.	Characterized by joking
_____ 14.	CALAMITY	N.	Extraordinarily great in size, extent, or degree; gigantic; huge
_____ 15.	ELUDE	O.	Indicating or showing unbelief; skeptical
_____ 16.	MEEK	P.	Unnatural or sickly pallor; pallid; lacking color
_____ 17.	WAN	Q.	Made or became slower; slowed down
_____ 18.	SLACKENED	R.	Unusually advanced or mature in development, esp. mentally
_____ 19.	GAUDY	S.	Overly submissive or compliant; spiritless; tame
_____ 20.	PHANTASM	T.	Unending

The Time Machine MULTIPLE CHOICE UNIT TEST 2 Answer Key

I. Matching/Identify

I	1. ELOI	A.	The Eloi were this to the Morlocks.
F	2. NARRATOR	B.	The very young man wanted to hear Greek from ______'s very lips.
P	3. MEDICAL	C.	She nearly drowned.
J	4. CRAB	D.	Giant white statue in the forest
D	5. SPHINX	E.	The Time Traveller's souvenir from the future; wilted ______
E	6. FLOWERS	F.	He kept the Time Traveller's souvenir from the future.
R	7. MATCHES	G.	Morlocks used this when cleaning the time machine.
O	8. EDITOR	H.	He found himself on a very strange adventure; the Time ______.
C	9. WEENA	I.	They had a peaceful, fruit-eating society.
Q	10. MORLOCKS	J.	It attacked the Time Traveller in the far future; giant ______.
A	11. MEAT	K.	He seemed to be the most nervous person in the room; the ______ Man
H	12. TRAVELLER	L.	The Time Traveller found this explosive in the museum
S	13. MUSEUM	M.	It was hidden inside the bronze pedestal.
M	14. MACHINE	N.	The Eloi survived on this food.
K	15. SILENT	O.	He was the first to speak after the lengthy tale.
B	16. PLATO	P.	He was instructed to begin dinner promptly at 7:00 P.M.; the ______ Man
L	17. DYNAMITE	Q.	Industrious, underground carnivores
G	18. OIL	R.	People of the future had not seen these before.
N	19. FRUIT	S.	The Palace of Green Porcelain
T	20. TIME	T.	The fourth dimension

B 1. What do the men see when the Psychologist presses the lever on the Time Machine model?
    A. Nothing happens.
    B. The model disappears before their eyes.
    C. The Time Machine explodes in a cloud of smoke.
    D. The Psychologist disappears before their eyes.

B 2. Who seems to become the most nervous when the Time Traveller sits down to dinner?
    A. The Medical Man
    B. The Silent Man
    C. The Psychologist
    D. The Narrator

D 3. What does the Time Traveller notice when he uses the machine for the very first time?
    A. The crystal needed to activate the machine is cracked.
    B. He feels like he is sleep walking.
    C. Nothing happens when he tries the machine the first time.
    D. The time on the clock goes from 10:01 to 3:30.

A 4. What does the Time Traveller see when he stops the machine in the garden?
    A. He sees a lawn surrounded by rhododendron bushes and a colossal white marble figure in the shape of a winged sphinx.
    B. He sees the moon and realizes it is too close to the earth.
    C. He sees a huge castle made of glass.
    D. He sees a small village in the distance, but no people.

B 5. What does the Time Traveller notice about the little people and their society?
    A. Both the men and the women are fierce hunters and warriors.
    B. No one seems to do any work. They eat fruit all day and sleep in communal houses.
    C. The people have superhuman intelligence and are able to move things with their minds.
    D. They are a contemplative society that spends days discussing philosophical issues.

A 6.   Although he is in great distress over the missing Time Machine, what one fact makes the Time Traveller feel reassured?

    A.   He has the levers to work the machine in his pocket.

    B.   He knew even if he could not get home, he would be very happy living with the little people.

    C.   He has the key to start the machine in his pocket.

    D.   He has the plans to the machine in his pocket and can build a new machine.

A 7.   What clue does the Time Traveller find that leads him to believe he knows the whereabouts of the Time Machine?

    A.   There are grooves and footprints in the dirt in front of the bronze pedestal.

    B.   He overhears a group of the people talking; they mention a cave in the forest.

    C.   There is a trail of broken parts leading into the forest.

    D.   There is a note in his pocket telling him the machine has been "borrowed."

D 8.   How do the Time Traveller and Weena become friends?

    A.   He asks her to serve as a guide into the wilderness as he looks for his Time Machine.

    B.   Weena's father gives her to the Time Traveller as a gift.

    C.   Weena feels pity for him because he is alone, so she hangs out with him.

    D.   The Time Traveller saves her from drowning.

A 9.   How does the Time Traveller describe the strange creature he encounters in a colossal ruin near the great hall?

    A.   He sees a dull white, ape-like creature with grayish-red eyes.

    B.   He sees a seven-foot man-like creature covered with fur.

    C.   He sees a great serpent with bright yellow eyes and huge fangs.

    D.   He sees a huge spider-like creature with large claws, long antennae, and many legs.

C 10.   What does the Time Traveller learn about the diet of the Morlocks?

    A.   They are vegetarians.

    B.   They only eat once a week.

    C.   They are carnivores.

    D.   They eat the rodents that live in their caves.

A 11.   What is the "clear knowledge" regarding the meat seen by the Time Traveller in the Morlocks' caverns?

   A.   The meat on the white table is an Eloi; the Morlocks eat them.

   B.   The Morlocks are cannibals; they eat each other.

   C.   The Morlocks use the meat to try to capture the giant serpent that lives underground.

   D.   The meat is placed there as bait to draw the Time Traveller into the caverns.

A 12.   What weapon does the Time Traveller believe would be the most effective against the Morlocks?

   A.   Fire

   B.   A mace

   C.   A crossbow

   D.   Dynamite

B 13.   What is the Palace of Green Porcelain?

   A.   It is the Time Traveller's own house.

   B.   It is an ancient museum.

   C.   It is an ancient bank.

   D.   It is an ancient train station.

D 14.   What does the Time Traveller find in one of the galleries that literally makes him dance?

   A.   He finds books that he himself had published about time travel.

   B.   He finds canned foods that were still good enough to eat.

   C.   He finds two workable sticks of dynamite.

   D.   He finds a box of matches.

D 15.   What does the Time Traveller do that he later discovers to be an "atrocious folly?"

   A.   He runs into the woods without first checking his whereabouts.

   B.   He leaves Weena unguarded near a hollow tree.

   C.   He throws the sticks of dynamite at the Morlocks.

   D.   He lights the firewood to frighten the Morlocks.

B 16.   What does the Time Traveller notice about the Time Machine when he finds it?

   A.   The dials are broken; he doesn't know if the machine will work.

   B.   The Morlocks have cleaned and oiled it thoroughly.

   C.   It is covered with a slimy film from being underground.

   D.   The crystal that makes it work is now cracked.

D 17.   How does the Time Traveller finally escape the Morlocks?

   A.   The Eloi come to his rescue and distract the Morlocks long enough for him to leave.

   B.   He throws a stick of dynamite at them and blows them up.

   C.   He lures them to a tunnel he has filled with gunpowder. He then sets off the charge, sealing the Morlocks inside.

   D.   He fights the Morlocks while he inserts the levers into the machine. He is able to turn it on and escape.

C 18.   When the Time Traveller stops again after escaping the Morlocks, what is the earth like?

   A.   It is more beautiful than the Time Traveller remembered.

   B.   It is cold and very dark.

   C.   It is a very dark, dismal place.

   D.   It is covered in water.

B 19.   What becomes of the Time Traveller?

   A.   He is so traumatized by his experiences that he destroys the time machine.

   B.   He enters the time machine once more and is never seen again.

   C.   He becomes world-famous for his invention.

   D.   He is committed to an insane asylum.

B 20.   What does the Narrator have as a reminder "that even when mind and strength had gone, gratitude and a mutual tenderness still lived in the heart of Man?"

   A.   The Narrator has become closer friends with the Time Traveller.

   B.   The Narrator has the two wilted flowers.

   C.   The Narrator has the miniature model of the time machine.

   D.   The Narrator has the Time Traveller's journal of his adventures.

IV. Vocabulary

O	1. INCREDULOUS	A.	In a condition or process of mental or moral decay
M	2. JOCULAR	B.	Avoid or escape by speed, cleverness, or trickery; to evade
C	3. ANECDOTES	C.	Short accounts of interesting or humorous incidents
N	4. COLOSSAL	D.	Showing a disposition to avoid exertion; slothful; lazy
F	5. FRUGIVOROUS	E.	Out of the ordinary course of nature; exceptionally or abnormally
D	6. INDOLENT	F.	Feeding on fruit; fruit eating
R	7. PRECOCIOUS	G.	A club-like armor-breaking weapon of war
K	8. INTIMATE	H.	Brilliantly or excessively showy
A	9. DECADENT	I.	Great misfortune or disaster
T	10. INTERMINABLE	J.	Compound used in the manufacture of plastics and explosives
E	11. PRETERNATURALLY	K.	To indicate or make known indirectly; hint; imply; suggest
G	12. MACE	L.	Creation of the imagination or fancy; fantasy
J	13. CAMPHOR	M.	Characterized by joking
I	14. CALAMITY	N.	Extraordinarily great in size, extent, or degree; gigantic; huge
B	15. ELUDE	O.	Indicating or showing unbelief; skeptical
S	16. MEEK	P.	Unnatural or sickly pallor; pallid; lacking color
P	17. WAN	Q.	Made or became slower; slowed down
Q	18. SLACKENED	R.	Unusually advanced or mature in development, esp. mentally
H	19. GAUDY	S.	Overly submissive or compliant; spiritless; tame
L	20. PHANTASM	T.	Unending

UNIT RESOURCE MATERIALS

1. Save one corner of the board for the best of students' *The Time Machine* writing assignments.

2. Take one of the word search puzzles from the extra activities packet and, with a marker, copy it over in a large size on the bulletin board. Write the clue words to find to one side. Invite students prior to and after class to find the words and circle them on the bulletin board.

3. Write several of the most significant quotations from the book onto the board on brightly colored paper.

4. Make a bulletin board listing the vocabulary words for this unit. As you complete sections of the novel and discuss the vocabulary for each section, write the definitions on the bulletin board. (If your board is one students face frequently, it will help them learn the words.)

5. Make a poster for each man who was invited to the Time Traveller's house for dinner. Include the speculations as to why each was invited.

6. Display the journal entries of the dinner guests written in class.

7. Create a display devoted to 19th Century scientific discoveries.

8. Draw a large map of the Eloi country and map out the Time Traveller's adventures in this place.

9. Display the posters from the scientific fiction authors projects.

10. Create a bulletin board devoted to the life of H. G. Wells.

11. Create a display of novels, television shows, and movies whose major theme is time travel.

12. Using textual evidence, create posters of the Eloi, the Morlocks, the Time Traveller, the crab creatures, and the tentacled creatures of the far distant future.

1. Time Travel
2. Retro sci-fi and current science
3. Producing a sci-fi show
4. Sci-fi network; trends in sci-fi shows
5. Transportation of the future
6. Inventions that will affect how we live in our homes in the future
7. The speed of change
8. Einstein's views on time
9. Black holes
10. Space exploration
11. Rockets and space vehicles
12. Popular modern-day science fiction books and movies
13. The technology of science fiction
14. Famous (and not so famous) inventions
15. Scientific Discoveries
16. Evolution
17. *War of the Worlds* by H. G. Wells
18. *The Island of Dr. Moreau* by H. G. Wells
19. *The Invisible Man* by H. G. Wells
20. Science Fiction Works by Jules Verne
21. Science Fiction Works by Ray Bradbury
22. Science Fiction Works by Pierre Boulle
23. Careers in science or technology
24. How to get an idea for an invention patented
25. UFOs

1. Watch an episode of the television show, *Quantum Leap* (available on DVD). You may also substitute scenes from any of the *Back to the Future* films as well, if you prefer. While students are watching, have them take notes on the original history of the time character Sam Becket leaps into, what needs to be changed, and how Sam goes about "putting right what once went wrong." Discuss these ideas after the video finishes.

2. Have students work together to make a time line of the main events of the story. Tape a large piece of butcher paper to one wall and have students write in the events directly onto the paper.

3. Have 3 students volunteer to be the Time Traveller. (Time Traveller #1, Time Traveller #2, and Time Traveller #3). They should sit on seats facing the class. Students in your class are "reporters." They should think of questions to ask the Time Traveller (choose to ask #1, #2, or #3). You are the moderator who chooses the order in which the reporters ask questions. The Time Travellers have to answer the questions as well as they can based on the facts in the book--and allowing for reasonable responses outside of the facts of the book based on the Time Traveller's character.

4. Have students make a list of the most useful things the Time Traveller needed in his travels. Have students suppose they were going to travel in time. Have them brainstorm a list of things they would take with them into the future. What would they take into the past?

5. Have students write a poem about Weena, either as Weena, as the Time Traveller, or as the narrator.

6. Have students draw plans for a time machine. It should include all parts students think would be necessary for successful time travel, and the parts should be labeled.

7. Assign students to 6 different groups, one for each reading assignment. Each group should turn its section of the book into a play script. If time permits, students could actually act out their sections of the book.

8. Have students write an essay or poem describing what time travel would feel like. They should use a first person point of view.

9. Have students forecast the future. What are their ideas about what the world will be like in 50 years, 100 years, 10,000 years? This could be a class discussion or a writing assignment.

10. What inventions of today influence our science fiction writers? Brainstorm a list with your students, and get their opinions about what possibilities these things open up that the discoveries in the 19th Century did not.

11. Hold a discussion about what time actually IS. Why do some minutes go by so slowly while others fly by? Why does time SEEM different at different times? Do your students believe time is in a constant line, or is it somehow parallel or in some other form?

12. Ask students why "old" science fiction movies and shows seem so "corny" to us today, whereas the science fiction movies and shows of our time seem exciting and hold our interest. Why is that? Have students work in small groups to come up with characters and a plot for a pilot for a new science fiction television show.

No.	Word	Clue/Definition
1.	BLANK	Editor's name
2.	CAMPHOR	Volatile substance the Time Traveller found in the museum
3.	CHOSE	Silent Man's name
4.	CLOCK	Goes from 10:01 to 3:20 in a matter of seconds
5.	CRAB	It attacked the Time Traveller in the far future; giant ______.
6.	DARKNESS	The Time Traveller dreaded this.
7.	DASH	Name of the Journalist
8.	DYNAMITE	The Time Traveller found this explosive in the museum
9.	EDITOR	He was the first to speak after the lengthy tale.
10.	ELOI	They had a peaceful, fruit-eating society.
11.	FILBY	Argumentative person with red hair
12.	FIRE	Morlocks feared it
13.	FLOWERS	The Time Traveller's souvenir from the future; wilted ______
14.	FRUIT	The Eloi survived on this food.
15.	GAZETTE	*Pall Mall* ___ comfirms the date the Time Traveller returns home.
16.	GROOVE	This was a clue as to where the time machine was hidden.
17.	LEVERS	The Time Traveller kept these in his pocket.
18.	MACHINE	It was hidden inside the bronze pedestal.
19.	MATCHES	People of the future had not seen these before.
20.	MEAT	The Eloi were this to the Morlocks.
21.	MEDICAL	He was instructed to begin dinner promptly at 7:00 P.M.; the ______ Man
22.	MORLOCKS	Industrious, underground carnivores
23.	MUSEUM	The Palace of Green Porcelain
24.	NARRATOR	He kept the Time Traveller's souvenir from the future.
25.	OIL	Morlocks used this when cleaning the time machine.
26.	PLATO	The very young man wanted to hear Greek from _____'s very lips.
27.	PSYCHOLOGIST	He presses the lever on the Time Machine model.
28.	RHODODENDRON	These surround the lawn where the Time Machine stops.
29.	RICHARDSON	Publisher the Time Traveller never got to meet with
30.	RICHMOND	Town in which the Time Traveller lives
31.	SALTPETER	The Time Traveller needs this to make gunpowder.
32.	SHOES	The Time Traveller threw these away when he was going through the forest with Weena.
33.	SILENT	He seemed to be the most nervous person in the room; the ______ Man
34.	SPHINX	Giant white statue in the forest
35.	STARS	These have repositioned themselves over time.

No.	Word	Clue/Definition
36.	SUN	Eloi believed that the Time Traveller came from this place.
37.	TIME	The fourth dimension
38.	TRAVELLER	He found himself on a very strange adventure; the Time ______.
39.	UTOPIA	The Time Traveller compared the Eloi society to this perfect society.
40.	WATCHETT	Time Traveller's housekeeper
41.	WEENA	She nearly drowned.

WORD SEARCH - Time Machine

```
M  X  S  U  N  E  Z  K  N  M  S  P  G  R  O  O  V  E  O  C
L  E  T  X  T  L  C  H  O  U  H  D  L  H  D  D  D  J  I  Y
M  G  A  W  M  O  Y  T  S  S  O  Y  F  A  G  I  M  C  L  Q
H  F  R  T  L  I  P  B  D  E  E  N  D  W  T  D  O  M  L  T
F  Z  S  C  E  T  T  I  R  U  S  A  M  O  N  O  R  L  K  Y
F  D  L  R  C  P  F  G  A  M  Y  M  R  D  O  H  L  G  R  T
P  G  I  K  V  S  C  M  H  N  F  I  Y  V  R  Y  O  C  Z  M
W  F  P  M  H  Y  A  J  C  V  T  T  V  H  D  Q  C  Z  J  Y
F  G  V  C  B  C  C  R  I  L  W  E  N  X  N  R  K  N  T  X
F  J  N  Q  H  H  G  S  R  K  F  L  O  W  E  R  S  Y  R  F
R  L  T  I  Q  O  B  F  A  S  J  N  Y  A  D  J  K  X  A  T
K  W  N  Q  R  L  L  Q  J  L  L  B  Q  T  O  T  C  M  V  K
M  E  Q  R  E  O  W  W  W  F  T  E  N  C  D  N  A  B  E  Y
L  E  Y  R  S  G  H  Y  E  B  R  P  V  H  O  E  M  L  L  K
V  D  D  G  O  I  G  M  H  F  Z  U  E  E  H  L  P  A  L  X
Z  F  W  I  H  S  I  Z  X  H  Z  Q  I  T  R  I  H  N  E  C
X  S  E  H  C  T  A  M  G  A  Z  E  T  T  E  S  O  K  R  D
C  N  A  R  R  A  T  O  R  Q  H  P  R  Y  A  R  R  A  W  N
W  E  E  N  A  Y  L  S  P  H  I  N  X  D  Q  Y  B  L  I  F
```

BLANK	GAZETTE	RHODODENDRON
CAMPHOR	GROOVE	RICHARDSON
CHOSE	LEVERS	SALTPETER
CLOCK	MACHINE	SHOES
CRAB	MATCHES	SILENT
DASH	MEAT	SPHINX
DYNAMITE	MEDICAL	STARS
EDITOR	MORLOCKS	SUN
ELOI	MUSEUM	TIME
FILBY	NARRATOR	TRAVELLER
FIRE	OIL	UTOPIA
FLOWERS	PLATO	WATCHETT
FRUIT	PSYCHOLOGIST	WEENA

WORD SEARCH ANSWER KEY - Time Machine

M   S   U   N   E   K   N   M   S   P   G   R   O   O   V   E   O
  E   T   T   L   C   O   U   H   D   L   A   I   D   I
    R   T   O   S   S   O   Y   A   T   M   O   L
    S   C   E   P   I   D   E   U   S   N   O   N   O   R   L
        R   P   I   R   U   S   A   M   R   O   R   L
    I   Y   M   H   C   I   R   O   C   T
F   P   A   I   T   D   K   R
            C   H   R   E   N   S   A
        H   O   S   R   F   L   O   W   E   R   S   V
      N   L   A   W   A   D   E   L
M   E   E   O   L   L   T   O   T   C   L
  E   S   G   F   T   E   C   D   N   A   B   E
    D   O   I   E   R   P   V   H   O   E   M   L   L
      I   H   S   I   U   E   E   H   L   P   A   E
S   E   H   C   T   A   M   G   A   Z   E   T   T   E   S   O   K   R   C
  N   A   R   R   A   T   O   R   A   R   R   A
W   E   E   N   A   L   S   P   H   I   N   X   D   Y   B   L   I   F

BLANK	GAZETTE	RHODODENDRON
CAMPHOR	GROOVE	RICHARDSON
CHOSE	LEVERS	SALTPETER
CLOCK	MACHINE	SHOES
CRAB	MATCHES	SILENT
DASH	MEAT	SPHINX
DYNAMITE	MEDICAL	STARS
EDITOR	MORLOCKS	SUN
ELOI	MUSEUM	TIME
FILBY	NARRATOR	TRAVELLER
FIRE	OIL	UTOPIA
FLOWERS	PLATO	WATCHETT
FRUIT	PSYCHOLOGIST	WEENA

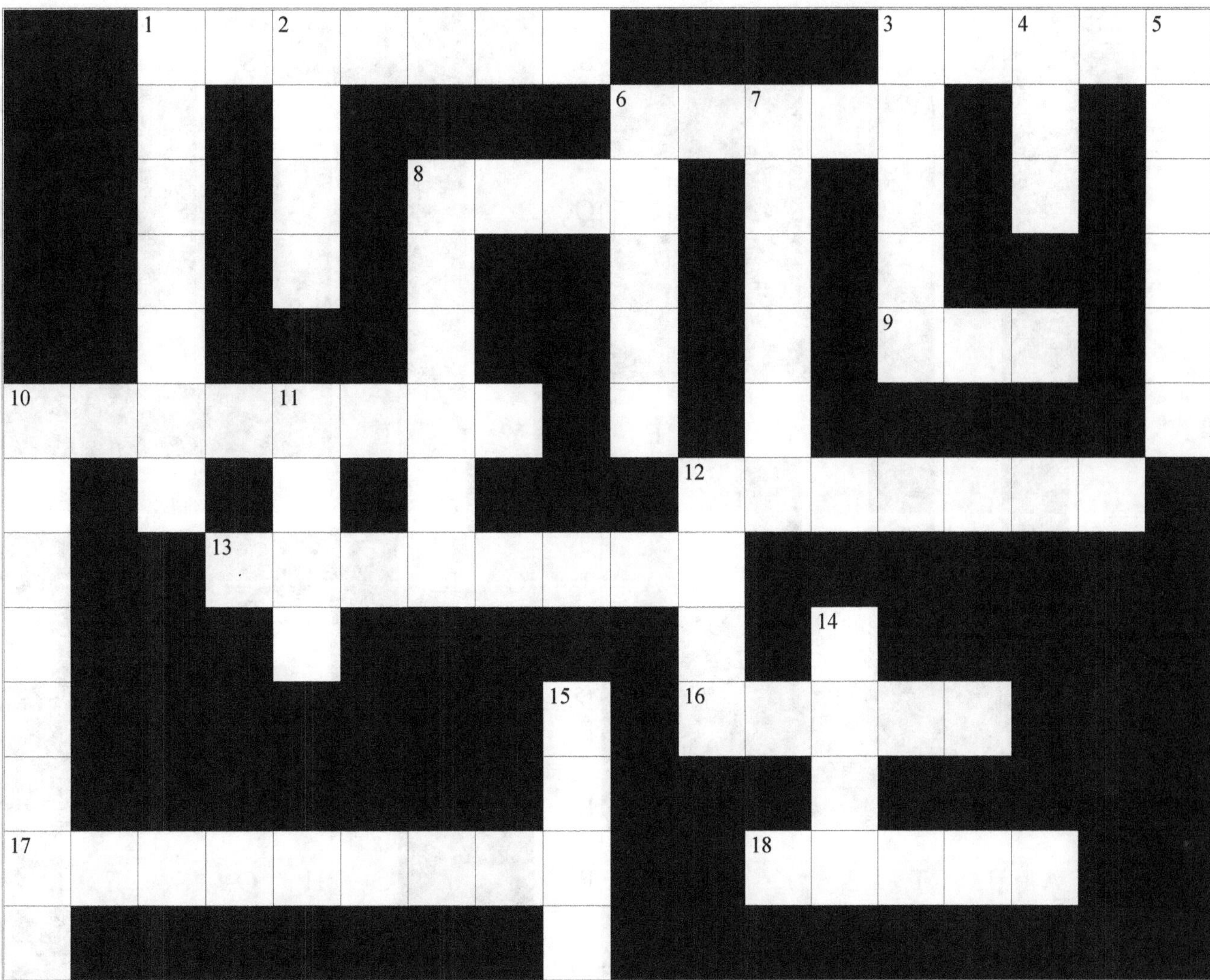

Across

1. People of the future had not seen these.
3. The Time Traveller threw these away when going through the forest with Weena.
6. Eloi survived on this food group.
8. They had a peaceful, fruit-eating society.
9. Eloi believed the Time Traveller came from this place.
10. Explosive the Time Traveller found in the museum
12. Volatile substance the Time Traveller found in the museum
13. He kept the Time Traveller's souvenir from the future.
16. Editor's name
17. The Time Traveller needs this to make gunpowder.
18. Silent Man's name

Down

1. It was hidden inside the bronze pedestal.
2. The fourth dimension
3. They repositioned themselves over time.
4. Morlocks used this when cleaning the time machine.
5. The most nervous person in the room; the ___ Man
6. Argumentative person with red hair
7. The Time Traveller compared the Eloi society to this.
8. He spoke first after the Traveller's tale.
10. The Time Traveller dreaded this.
11. Eloi were this to the Morlocks.
12. It attacked the Time Traveller in the far future; giant ___.
14. Name of the Journalist
15. Morlocks feared it.

Across

1. People of the future had not seen these.
3. The Time Traveller threw these away when going through the forest with Weena.
6. Eloi survived on this food group.
8. They had a peaceful, fruit-eating society.
9. Eloi believed the Time Traveller came from this place.
10. Explosive the Time Traveller found in the museum
12. Volatile substance the Time Traveller found in the museum
13. He kept the Time Traveller's souvenir from the future.
16. Editor's name
17. The Time Traveller needs this to make gunpowder.
18. Silent Man's name

Down

1. It was hidden inside the bronze pedestal.
2. The fourth dimension
3. They repositioned themselves over time.
4. Morlocks used this when cleaning the time machine.
5. The most nervous person in the room; the ___ Man
6. Argumentative person with red hair
7. The Time Traveller compared the Eloi society to this.
8. He spoke first after the Traveller's tale.
10. The Time Traveller dreaded this.
11. Eloi were this to the Morlocks.
12. It attacked the Time Traveller in the far future; giant ___.
14. Name of the Journalist
15. Morlocks feared it.

MATCHING 1 *The Time Machine*

____	1.	ELOI	A.	This was a clue as to where the time machine was hidden.
____	2.	FIRE	B.	Giant white statue in the forest
____	3.	CAMPHOR	C.	The Time Traveller threw these away when he was going through the forest with Weena.
____	4.	DYNAMITE	D.	Morlocks used this when cleaning the time machine.
____	5.	OIL	E.	The Time Traveller's souvenir from the future; wilted ________
____	6.	SHOES	F.	Morlocks feared it
____	7.	LEVERS	G.	The Palace of Green Porcelain
____	8.	UTOPIA	H.	Editor's name
____	9.	PSYCHOLOGIST	I.	The Time Traveller found this explosive in the museum
____	10.	DASH	J.	He presses the lever on the Time Machine model.
____	11.	MEDICAL	K.	The Time Traveller compared the Eloi society to this perfect society.
____	12.	SPHINX	L.	He was instructed to begin dinner promptly at 7:00 P.M.; the _______ Man
____	13.	FLOWERS	M.	Industrious, underground carnivores
____	14.	MORLOCKS	N.	The Time Traveller kept these in his pocket.
____	15.	MUSEUM	O.	He seemed to be the most nervous person in the room; the _______ Man
____	16.	SILENT	P.	Volatile substance the Time Traveller found in the museum
____	17.	WATCHETT	Q.	They had a peaceful, fruit-eating society.
____	18.	BLANK	R.	Time Traveller's housekeeper
____	19.	GROOVE	S.	Name of the Journalist

Q	1. ELOI	A. This was a clue as to where the time machine was hidden.
F	2. FIRE	B. Giant white statue in the forest
P	3. CAMPHOR	C. The Time Traveller threw these away when he was going through the forest with Weena.
I	4. DYNAMITE	D. Morlocks used this when cleaning the time machine.
D	5. OIL	E. The Time Traveller's souvenir from the future; wilted ______
C	6. SHOES	F. Morlocks feared it
N	7. LEVERS	G. The Palace of Green Porcelain
K	8. UTOPIA	H. Editor's name
J	9. PSYCHOLOGIST	I. The Time Traveller found this explosive in the museum
S	10. DASH	J. He presses the lever on the Time Machine model.
L	11. MEDICAL	K. The Time Traveller compared the Eloi society to this perfect society.
B	12. SPHINX	L. He was instructed to begin dinner promptly at 7:00 P.M.; the ______ Man
E	13. FLOWERS	M. Industrious, underground carnivores
M	14. MORLOCKS	N. The Time Traveller kept these in his pocket.
G	15. MUSEUM	O. He seemed to be the most nervous person in the room; the ______ Man
O	16. SILENT	P. Volatile substance the Time Traveller found in the museum
R	17. WATCHETT	Q. They had a peaceful, fruit-eating society.
H	18. BLANK	R. Time Traveller's housekeeper
A	19. GROOVE	S. Name of the Journalist

_____ 1.	ELOI	A.	Morlocks feared it
_____ 2.	FILBY	B.	The Time Traveller found this explosive in the museum
_____ 3.	FIRE	C.	Publisher the Time Traveller never got to meet with
_____ 4.	DYNAMITE	D.	Eloi believed that the Time Traveller came from this place.
_____ 5.	SHOES	E.	He found himself on a very strange adventure; the Time ______.
_____ 6.	RICHMOND	F.	The Time Traveller kept these in his pocket.
_____ 7.	LEVERS	G.	They had a peaceful, fruit-eating society.
_____ 8.	SUN	H.	Time Traveller's housekeeper
_____ 9.	FRUIT	I.	The Time Traveller's souvenir from the future; wilted ______
_____ 10.	PLATO	J.	It attacked the Time Traveller in the far future; giant ______.
_____ 11.	WATCHETT	K.	The Eloi survived on this food.
_____ 12.	CRAB	L.	He was the first to speak after the lengthy tale.
_____ 13.	FLOWERS	M.	Argumentative person with red hair
_____ 14.	EDITOR	N.	Town in which the Time Traveller lives
_____ 15.	MEAT	O.	He seemed to be the most nervous person in the room; the ______ Man
_____ 16.	TRAVELLER	P.	The Time Traveller compared the Eloi society to this perfect society.
_____ 17.	SILENT	Q.	The very young man wanted to hear Greek from ______'s very lips.
_____ 18.	RICHARDSON	R.	The Time Traveller threw these away when he was going through the forest with Weena.
_____ 19.	CHOSE	S.	The Eloi were this to the Morlocks.
_____ 20.	UTOPIA	T.	Silent Man's name

G	1. ELOI	A.	Morlocks feared it
M	2. FILBY	B.	The Time Traveller found this explosive in the museum
A	3. FIRE	C.	Publisher the Time Traveller never got to meet with
B	4. DYNAMITE	D.	Eloi believed that the Time Traveller came from this place.
R	5. SHOES	E.	He found himself on a very strange adventure; the Time _____.
N	6. RICHMOND	F.	The Time Traveller kept these in his pocket.
F	7. LEVERS	G.	They had a peaceful, fruit-eating society.
D	8. SUN	H.	Time Traveller's housekeeper
K	9. FRUIT	I.	The Time Traveller's souvenir from the future; wilted ______
Q	10. PLATO	J.	It attacked the Time Traveller in the far future; giant _______.
H	11. WATCHETT	K.	The Eloi survived on this food.
J	12. CRAB	L.	He was the first to speak after the lengthy tale.
I	13. FLOWERS	M.	Argumentative person with red hair
L	14. EDITOR	N.	Town in which the Time Traveller lives
S	15. MEAT	O.	He seemed to be the most nervous person in the room; the ______ Man
E	16. TRAVELLER	P.	The Time Traveller compared the Eloi society to this perfect society.
O	17. SILENT	Q.	The very young man wanted to hear Greek from _____'s very lips.
C	18. RICHARDSON	R.	The Time Traveller threw these away when he was going through the forest with Weena.
T	19. CHOSE	S.	The Eloi were this to the Morlocks.
P	20. UTOPIA	T.	Silent Man's name

______________	= 1. LOEI They had a peaceful, fruit-eating society.
______________	= 2. MECNAHI It was hidden inside the bronze pedestal.
______________	= 3. UMUMSE The Palace of Green Porcelain
______________	= 4. RLVEALTRE He found himself on a very strange adventure; the Time _____.
______________	= 5. EMAT The Eloi were this to the Morlocks.
______________	= 6. ORKMOLCS Industrious, underground carnivores
______________	= 7. WNAEE She nearly drowned.
______________	= 8. TEDRIO He was the first to speak after the lengthy tale.
______________	= 9. TESACHM People of the future had not seen these before.
______________	= 10. FESORLW The Time Traveller's souvenir from the future; wilted ______
______________	= 11. NXPSHI Giant white statue in the forest
______________	= 12. RCAB It attacked the Time Traveller in the far future; giant ______.
______________	= 13. ALEDICM He was instructed to begin dinner promptly at 7:00 P.M.; the ______ Man
______________	= 14. RARTAONR He kept the Time Traveller's souvenir from the future.
______________	= 15. ISNELT He seemed to be the most nervous person in the room; the ______ Man

ELOI   = 1. LOEI
                         They had a peaceful, fruit-eating society.

MACHINE   = 2. MECNAHI
                         It was hidden inside the bronze pedestal.

MUSEUM   = 3. UMUMSE
                         The Palace of Green Porcelain

TRAVELLER   = 4. RLVEALTRE
                         He found himself on a very strange adventure; the Time _____.

MEAT   = 5. EMAT
                         The Eloi were this to the Morlocks.

MORLOCKS   = 6. ORKMOLCS
                         Industrious, underground carnivores

WEENA   = 7. WNAEE
                         She nearly drowned.

EDITOR   = 8. TEDRIO
                         He was the first to speak after the lengthy tale.

MATCHES   = 9. TESACHM
                         People of the future had not seen these before.

FLOWERS   = 10. FESORLW
                         The Time Traveller's souvenir from the future; wilted ______

SPHINX   = 11. NXPSHI
                         Giant white statue in the forest

CRAB   = 12. RCAB
                         It attacked the Time Traveller in the far future; giant ______.

MEDICAL   = 13. ALEDICM
                         He was instructed to begin dinner promptly at 7:00 P.M.; the ______
                         Man

NARRATOR   = 14. RARTAONR
                         He kept the Time Traveller's souvenir from the future.

SILENT   = 15. ISNELT
                         He seemed to be the most nervous person in the room; the ______ Man

_______________ = 1. SHDA
Name of the Journalist

_______________ = 2. APOTIU
The Time Traveller compared the Eloi society to this perfect society.

_______________ = 3. IRUFT
The Eloi survived on this food.

_______________ = 4. SNU
Eloi believed that the Time Traveller came from this place.

_______________ = 5. RSVELE
The Time Traveller kept these in his pocket.

_______________ = 6. IOCRHMDN
Town in which the Time Traveller lives

_______________ = 7. SOEHS
The Time Traveller threw these away when he was going through the forest with Weena.

_______________ = 8. OLI
Morlocks used this when cleaning the time machine.

_______________ = 9. DMTNAIYE
The Time Traveller found this explosive in the museum

_______________ = 10. AORCMHP
Volatile substance the Time Traveller found in the museum

_______________ = 11. EIFR
Morlocks feared it

_______________ = 12. LSISYTPHOCGO
He presses the lever on the Time Machine model.

_______________ = 13. YBILF
Argumentative person with red hair

_______________ = 14. RVGEOO
This was a clue as to where the time machine was hidden.

DASH   = 1.   SHDA
                               Name of the Journalist

UTOPIA   = 2.   APOTIU
                               The Time Traveller compared the Eloi society to this perfect society.

FRUIT   = 3.   IRUFT
                               The Eloi survived on this food.

SUN   = 4.   SNU
                               Eloi believed that the Time Traveller came from this place.

LEVERS   = 5.   RSVELE
                               The Time Traveller kept these in his pocket.

RICHMOND   = 6.   IOCRHMDN
                               Town in which the Time Traveller lives

SHOES   = 7.   SOEHS
                               The Time Traveller threw these away when he was going through
                               the forest with Weena.

OIL   = 8.   OLI
                               Morlocks used this when cleaning the time machine.

DYNAMITE   = 9.   DMTNAIYE
                               The Time Traveller found this explosive in the museum

CAMPHOR   = 10. AORCMHP
                               Volatile substance the Time Traveller found in the museum

FIRE   = 11. EIFR
                               Morlocks feared it

PSYCHOLOGIST   = 12. LSISYTPHOCGO
                               He presses the lever on the Time Machine model.

FILBY   = 13. YBILF
                               Argumentative person with red hair

GROOVE   = 14. RVGEOO
                               This was a clue as to where the time machine was hidden.

VOCABULARY RESOURCE MATERIALS

The Time Machine Vocabulary

No.	Word	Clue/Definition
1.	ABOMINATIONS	Things that cause a sense of disgust
2.	ACACIAS	Fragrant yellow flowers used in making perfumes
3.	ALGAL	Relating to algae
4.	AMELIORATING	Making better, more bearable, or more satisfactory; improving
5.	ANACHRONISMS	Persons, objects, or practices that belong to a different time period
6.	ANECDOTES	Short accounts of interesting or humorous incidents
7.	APERTURE	An opening, as a hole, slit, crack or gap
8.	ATTENUATED	To make thin; to make slender or fine
9.	BEGRIMED	Dirty
10.	BOLE	Stem or trunk of a tree
11.	CALAMITY	Great misfortune or disaster
12.	CAMPHOR	Compound used in the manufacture of plastics and explosives
13.	COLOSSAL	Extraordinarily great in size, extent, or degree; gigantic; huge
14.	COMPENSATION	Given or received in return for services, debt, injury, lack, etc.
15.	CONTRIVANCE	A device or control that is very useful for a particular job
16.	CUPOLAS	Small domes set on a round base or resting on pillars
17.	DECADENT	In a condition or process of mental or moral decay
18.	DELIQUESCED	Became liquid by absorbing moisture from the air, as certain salts
19.	DILAPIDATED	Fallen into partial ruin or decay, as from age, wear, or neglect
20.	EDDYING	Swirling as if in a whirlpool
21.	EKING	Getting with great effort or strain
22.	ELUDE	Avoid or escape by speed, cleverness, or trickery; to evade
23.	FRUGIVOROUS	Feeding on fruit; fruit eating
24.	GAUDY	Brilliantly or excessively showy
25.	IMPARTIALITY	Showing no bias; neutrality
26.	IMPEDED	Slowed or obstructed the progress of
27.	INARTICULATE	Lacking the ability to express oneself, esp. in clear speech
28.	INCREDULOUS	Indicating or showing unbelief; skeptical
29.	INDOLENT	Showing a disposition to avoid exertion; slothful; lazy
30.	INTERMINABLE	Unending
31.	INTIMATE	To indicate or make known indirectly; hint; imply; suggest
32.	JOCULAR	Characterized by joking
33.	MACE	A club-like armor-breaking weapon of war
34.	MEEK	Overly submissive or compliant; spiritless; tame

No.	Word	Clue/Definition
35.	MUTTON	The meat of sheep
36.	PALLID	Pale; faint or deficient in color
37.	PEPTONE	Complex water-soluble nutrient obtained by digesting protein
38.	PHANTASM	Creation of the imagination or fancy; fantasy
39.	POIGNANT	Affecting or moving the emotions
40.	PRECESSIONAL	The slow, conical motion of the earth's axis of rotation
41.	PRECOCIOUS	Unusually advanced or mature in development, esp. mentally
42.	PRETERNATURALLY	Out of the ordinary course of nature; exceptionally or abnormally
43.	PRODIGIOUS	Extraordinary in size, amount, extent, degree, force, etc.
44.	RECEDED	Moved away; retreated; withdrew
45.	RECONDITE	Dealing with very profound or difficult subject matter
46.	RILL	Small brook; rivulet
47.	SAURIANS	Lizards or similar reptiles
48.	SHOAL	Sandbank or sand bar in a body of water exposed at low tide
49.	SLACKENED	Made or became slower; slowed down
50.	SPECTRAL	Ghostly
51.	SUCCULENT	Full of juice; juicy
52.	TEMERITY	Reckless boldness; rashness
53.	TETHERED	Confined or restricted with or as if with a rope or chain
54.	TRUNCATED	Shortened by or as if by having a part cut off; cut short
55.	TUMULT	Highly distressing agitation of mind or feeling
56.	VELOCITY	Rapidity of motion or operation; swiftness; speed
57.	VERDIGRIS	A blue-green crust formed on copper, brass, or bronze surfaces exposed to the atmosphere for long periods of time
58.	WAN	Unnatural or sickly pallor; pallid; lacking color
59.	WHIM	Odd or capricious notion or desire; a sudden or freakish fancy

```
R  Q  R  F  K  D  A  I  K  J  W  S  K  K  A  S  P  L  T  W
B  N  E  Q  M  D  G  N  N  V  S  N  S  Y  C  A  L  G  M  J
E  D  C  F  W  N  N  Q  E  T  Q  Y  H  H  A  U  A  A  M  V
G  E  O  M  I  E  A  D  F  C  I  D  S  E  C  R  S  U  E  X
R  C  N  Y  R  K  M  T  Y  G  D  M  N  Y  I  I  S  D  E  Y
I  A  D  Y  F  I  T  T  T  S  H  O  A  L  A  A  O  Y  K  T
M  D  I  Z  H  N  C  N  I  E  T  W  T  T  S  N  L  Z  B  P
E  E  T  W  V  G  E  K  R  P  N  K  T  E  E  S  O  G  L  Q
D  N  E  Y  T  L  M  S  E  C  C  U  H  M  S  Y  C  K  A  K
B  T  J  N  U  M  S  P  M  C  A  L  A  M  I  T  Y  S  N  L
O  D  A  C  L  A  A  E  E  P  M  P  D  T  D  B  L  L  O  G
L  W  C  X  L  C  T  C  T  A  P  T  E  F  E  J  N  A  I  J
E  U  J  O  I  E  N  T  U  L  H  E  D  R  C  D  J  C  S  B
S  N  P  R  R  X  A  R  M  L  O  T  E  B  T  F  Y  K  S  M
B  U  H  G  E  R  H  A  U  I  R  H  P  K  K  U  Q  E  E  C
C  K  B  N  L  W  P  L  L  D  M  E  M  X  N  K  R  N  C  Z
H  T  T  R  U  N  C  A  T  E  D  R  I  F  W  C  J  E  E  L
W  W  X  J  D  S  U  O  L  U  D  E  R  C  N  I  W  D  R  H
D  Z  X  R  E  C  E  D  E  D  K  D  M  U  T  T  O  N  P  T
```

ACACIAS	CUPOLAS	MEEK	SHOAL
ALGAL	DECADENT	MUTTON	SLACKENED
ANECDOTES	EDDYING	PALLID	SPECTRAL
APERTURE	EKING	PEPTONE	SUCCULENT
ATTENUATED	ELUDE	PHANTASM	TEMERITY
BEGRIMED	GAUDY	PRECESSIONAL	TETHERED
BOLE	IMPEDED	RECEDED	TRUNCATED
CALAMITY	INCREDULOUS	RECONDITE	TUMULT
CAMPHOR	INTIMATE	RILL	WAN
COLOSSAL	MACE	SAURIANS	WHIM

VOCABULARY WORD SEARCH ANSWER KEY - Time Machine

ACACIAS	CUPOLAS	MEEK	SHOAL
ALGAL	DECADENT	MUTTON	SLACKENED
ANECDOTES	EDDYING	PALLID	SPECTRAL
APERTURE	EKING	PEPTONE	SUCCULENT
ATTENUATED	ELUDE	PHANTASM	TEMERITY
BEGRIMED	GAUDY	PRECESSIONAL	TETHERED
BOLE	IMPEDED	RECEDED	TRUNCATED
CALAMITY	INCREDULOUS	RECONDITE	TUMULT
CAMPHOR	INTIMATE	RILL	WAN
COLOSSAL	MACE	SAURIANS	WHIM

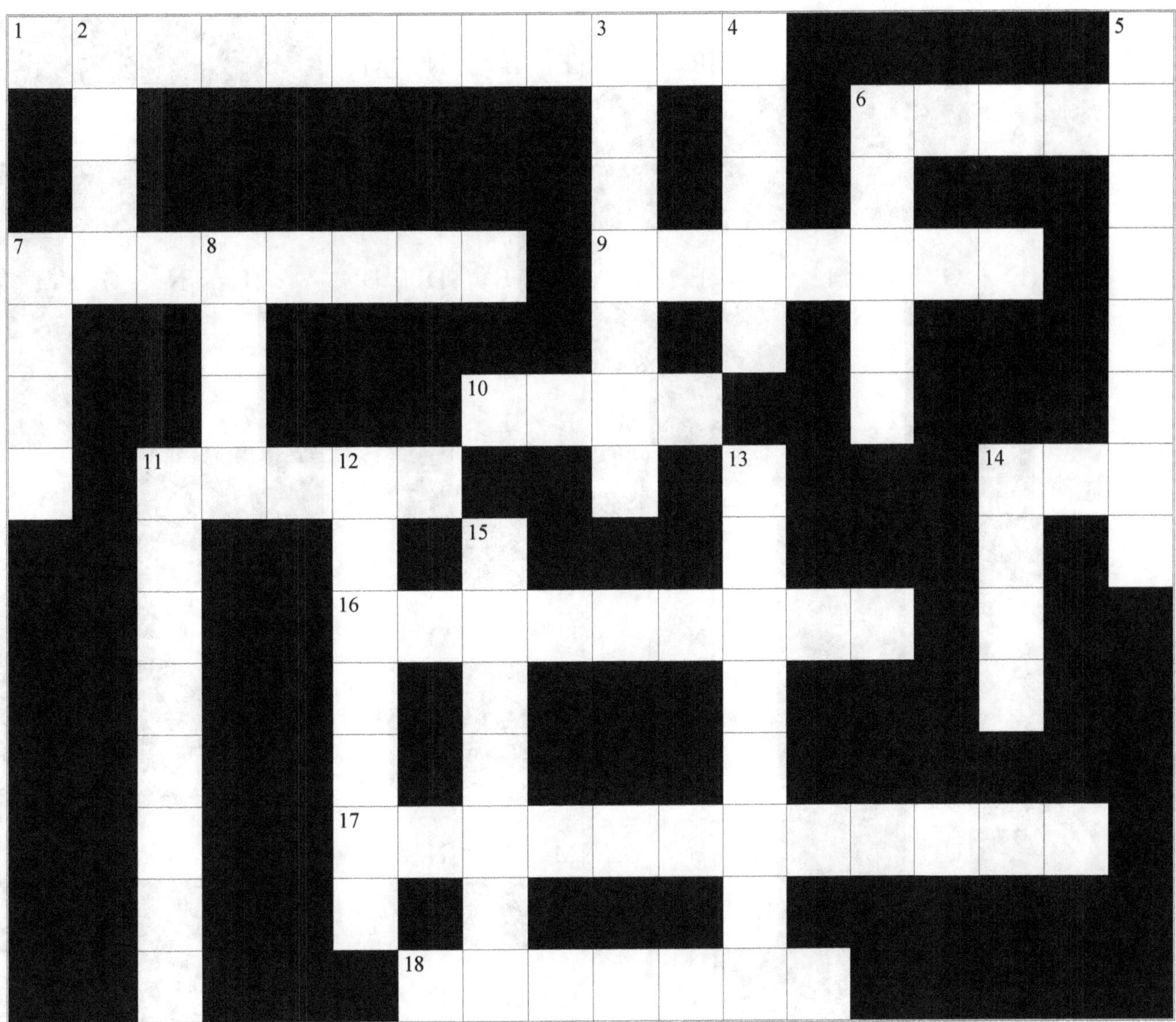

Across

1. Making better, more bearable, or more satisfactory
6. Avoid or escape by speed, cleverness or trickery
7. Dirty
9. Swirling as if in a whirlpool
10. Overly submissive or compliant; spiritless; tame
11. Relating to algae
14. Unnatural or sickly pallor; pallid; lacking color
16. Short accounts of interesting or humorous incidents
17. Things that cause a sense of disgust
18. Moved away from; retreated; withdrew

Down

2. Club-like, armor-breaking weapon of war
3. Slowed or obstructed the progress of
4. Brilliantly or excessively showy
5. In a condition or process of mental or moral decay
6. Getting with great effort or strain
7. Stem or trunk of a tree
8. Small brook; rivulet
11. Opening, as a hole, slit, crack, or gap
12. Fragrant yellow flowers used in perfumes
13. To indicate or make known indirectly; hint; imply; suggest
14. Odd or capricious notion or desire; a sudden fancy
15. Complex water-soluble nutrient obtained by digesting protein

Across

1. Making better, more bearable, or more satisfactory
6. Avoid or escape by speed, cleverness or trickery
7. Dirty
9. Swirling as if in a whirlpool
10. Overly submissive or compliant; spiritless; tame
11. Relating to algae
14. Unnatural or sickly pallor; pallid; lacking color
16. Short accounts of interesting or humorous incidents
17. Things that cause a sense of disgust
18. Moved away from; retreated; withdrew

Down

2. Club-like, armor-breaking weapon of war
3. Slowed or obstructed the progress of
4. Brilliantly or excessively showy
5. In a condition or process of mental or moral decay
6. Getting with great effort or strain
7. Stem or trunk of a tree
8. Small brook; rivulet
11. Opening, as a hole, slit, crack, or gap
12. Fragrant yellow flowers used in perfumes
13. To indicate or make known indirectly; hint; imply; suggest
14. Odd or capricious notion or desire; a sudden fancy
15. Complex water-soluble nutrient obtained by digesting protein

____ 1.	ABOMINATIONS	A.	Persons, objects, or practices that belong to a different time period
____ 2.	PHANTASM	B.	Shortened by or as if by having a part cut off; cut short
____ 3.	PRECESSIONAL	C.	A blue-green crust formed on copper, brass, or bronze surfaces exposed to the atmosphere for long periods of time
____ 4.	PRECOCIOUS	D.	The slow, conical motion of the earth's axis of rotation
____ 5.	PRODIGIOUS	E.	A device or control that is very useful for a particular job
____ 6.	SHOAL	F.	Unnatural or sickly pallor; pallid; lacking color
____ 7.	TEMERITY	G.	Characterized by joking
____ 8.	TRUNCATED	H.	The meat of sheep
____ 9.	VERDIGRIS	I.	Creation of the imagination or fancy; fantasy
____ 10.	MUTTON	J.	Great misfortune or disaster
____ 11.	JOCULAR	K.	Feeding on fruit; fruit eating
____ 12.	ANACHRONISMS	L.	Sandbank or sand bar in a body of water exposed at low tide
____ 13.	ATTENUATED	M.	Reckless boldness; rashness
____ 14.	CALAMITY	N.	Things that cause a sense of disgust
____ 15.	CONTRIVANCE	O.	Slowed or obstructed the progress of
____ 16.	DILAPIDATED	P.	Unusually advanced or mature in development, esp. mentally
____ 17.	FRUGIVOROUS	Q.	Showing a disposition to avoid exertion; slothful; lazy
____ 18.	IMPEDED	R.	To make thin; to make slender or fine
____ 19.	INDOLENT	S.	Fallen into partial ruin or decay, as from age, wear, or neglect
____ 20.	WAN	T.	Extraordinary in size, amount, extent, degree, force, etc.

N	1. ABOMINATIONS	A.	Persons, objects, or practices that belong to a different time period
I	2. PHANTASM	B.	Shortened by or as if by having a part cut off; cut short
D	3. PRECESSIONAL	C.	A blue-green crust formed on copper, brass, or bronze surfaces exposed to the atmosphere for long periods of time
P	4. PRECOCIOUS	D.	The slow, conical motion of the earth's axis of rotation
T	5. PRODIGIOUS	E.	A device or control that is very useful for a particular job
L	6. SHOAL	F.	Unnatural or sickly pallor; pallid; lacking color
M	7. TEMERITY	G.	Characterized by joking
B	8. TRUNCATED	H.	The meat of sheep
C	9. VERDIGRIS	I.	Creation of the imagination or fancy; fantasy
H	10. MUTTON	J.	Great misfortune or disaster
G	11. JOCULAR	K.	Feeding on fruit; fruit eating
A	12. ANACHRONISMS	L.	Sandbank or sand bar in a body of water exposed at low tide
R	13. ATTENUATED	M.	Reckless boldness; rashness
J	14. CALAMITY	N.	Things that cause a sense of disgust
E	15. CONTRIVANCE	O.	Slowed or obstructed the progress of
S	16. DILAPIDATED	P.	Unusually advanced or mature in development, esp. mentally
K	17. FRUGIVOROUS	Q.	Showing a disposition to avoid exertion; slothful; lazy
O	18. IMPEDED	R.	To make thin; to make slender or fine
Q	19. INDOLENT	S.	Fallen into partial ruin or decay, as from age, wear, or neglect
F	20. WAN	T.	Extraordinary in size, amount, extent, degree, force, etc.

_____ 1.	ACACIAS	A. Making better, more bearable, or more satisfactory; improving
_____ 2.	JOCULAR	B. Small brook; rivulet
_____ 3.	MEEK	C. Showing a disposition to avoid exertion; slothful; lazy
_____ 4.	PALLID	D. Ghostly
_____ 5.	POIGNANT	E. Small domes set on a round base or resting on pillars
_____ 6.	PRODIGIOUS	F. Lizards or similar reptiles
_____ 7.	RILL	G. Characterized by joking
_____ 8.	SAURIANS	H. Showing no bias; neutrality
_____ 9.	SPECTRAL	I. Became liquid by absorbing moisture from the air, as certain salts
_____ 10.	INDOLENT	J. Getting with great effort or strain
_____ 11.	IMPARTIALITY	K. Compound used in the manufacture of plastics and explosives
_____ 12.	AMELIORATING	L. Fragrant yellow flowers used in making perfumes
_____ 13.	ANECDOTES	M. Pale; faint or deficient in color
_____ 14.	BEGRIMED	N. Short accounts of interesting or humorous incidents
_____ 15.	CAMPHOR	O. Extraordinary in size, amount, extent, degree, force, etc.
_____ 16.	CUPOLAS	P. Dirty
_____ 17.	DELIQUESCED	Q. Highly distressing agitation of mind or feeling
_____ 18.	EDDYING	R. Swirling as if in a whirlpool
_____ 19.	EKING	S. Affecting or moving the emotions
_____ 20.	TUMULT	T. Overly submissive or compliant; spiritless; tame

VOCABULARY MATCHING 2 ANSWER KEY *The Time Machine*

L	1. ACACIAS	A.	Making better, more bearable, or more satisfactory; improving
G	2. JOCULAR	B.	Small brook; rivulet
T	3. MEEK	C.	Showing a disposition to avoid exertion; slothful; lazy
M	4. PALLID	D.	Ghostly
S	5. POIGNANT	E.	Small domes set on a round base or resting on pillars
O	6. PRODIGIOUS	F.	Lizards or similar reptiles
B	7. RILL	G.	Characterized by joking
F	8. SAURIANS	H.	Showing no bias; neutrality
D	9. SPECTRAL	I.	Became liquid by absorbing moisture from the air, as certain salts
C	10. INDOLENT	J.	Getting with great effort or strain
H	11. IMPARTIALITY	K.	Compound used in the manufacture of plastics and explosives
A	12. AMELIORATING	L.	Fragrant yellow flowers used in making perfumes
N	13. ANECDOTES	M.	Pale; faint or deficient in color
P	14. BEGRIMED	N.	Short accounts of interesting or humorous incidents
K	15. CAMPHOR	O.	Extraordinary in size, amount, extent, degree, force, etc.
E	16. CUPOLAS	P.	Dirty
I	17. DELIQUESCED	Q.	Highly distressing agitation of mind or feeling
R	18. EDDYING	R.	Swirling as if in a whirlpool
J	19. EKING	S.	Affecting or moving the emotions
Q	20. TUMULT	T.	Overly submissive or compliant; spiritless; tame

_______________ = 1. AAGLL
Relating to algae

_______________ = 2. EDDECRE
Moved away; retreated; withdrew

_______________ = 3. IRLL
Small brook; rivulet

_______________ = 4. LCDESKANE
Made or became slower; slowed down

_______________ = 5. LSTAPCER
Ghostly

_______________ = 6. DRHETETE
Confined or restricted with or as if with a rope or chain

_______________ = 7. UUTMLT
Highly distressing agitation of mind or feeling

_______________ = 8. TOVLCEYI
Rapidity of motion or operation; swiftness; speed

_______________ = 9. SIIVGRRED
A blue-green crust formed on copper, brass, or bronze surfaces
exposed to the atmosphere for long periods of time

_______________ = 10. PTUTEAERRALLRYN
Out of the ordinary course of nature; exceptionally or abnormally

_______________ = 11. SIRLOPAENCES
The slow, conical motion of the earth's axis of rotation

_______________ = 12. URAETPRE
An opening, as a hole, slit, crack or gap

_______________ = 13. ELOB
Stem or trunk of a tree

_______________ = 14. CPRMHAO
Compound used in the manufacture of plastics and explosives

_______________ = 15. GIDEDNY
Swirling as if in a whirlpool

_______________ = 16. YAGDU
Brilliantly or excessively showy

_______________ = 17. ITNERLNAMEBI
Unending

_______________ = 18. UOMTNT
The meat of sheep

_______________ = 19. SAHTNAMP
Creation of the imagination or fancy; fantasy

_______________ = 20. IWMH
Odd or capricious notion or desire; a sudden or freakish fancy

ALGAL = 1. AAGLL
Relating to algae

RECEDED = 2. EDDECRE
Moved away; retreated; withdrew

RILL = 3. IRLL
Small brook; rivulet

SLACKENED = 4. LCDESKANE
Made or became slower; slowed down

SPECTRAL = 5. LSTAPCER
Ghostly

TETHERED = 6. DRHETETE
Confined or restricted with or as if with a rope or chain

TUMULT = 7. UUTMLT
Highly distressing agitation of mind or feeling

VELOCITY = 8. TOVLCEYI
Rapidity of motion or operation; swiftness; speed

VERDIGRIS = 9. SIIVGRRED
A blue-green crust formed on copper, brass, or bronze surfaces exposed to the atmosphere for long periods of time

PRETERNATURALLY = 10. PTUTEAERRALLRYN
Out of the ordinary course of nature; exceptionally or abnormally

PRECESSIONAL = 11. SIRLOPAENCES
The slow, conical motion of the earth's axis of rotation

APERTURE = 12. URAETPRE
An opening, as a hole, slit, crack or gap

BOLE = 13. ELOB
Stem or trunk of a tree

CAMPHOR = 14. CPRMHAO
Compound used in the manufacture of plastics and explosives

EDDYING = 15. GIDEDNY
Swirling as if in a whirlpool

GAUDY = 16. YAGDU
Brilliantly or excessively showy

INTERMINABLE = 17. ITNERLNAMEBI
Unending

MUTTON = 18. UOMTNT
The meat of sheep

PHANTASM = 19. SAHTNAMP
Creation of the imagination or fancy; fantasy

WHIM = 20. IWMH
Odd or capricious notion or desire; a sudden or freakish fancy

__________ = 1. NNIMATIAOOBS
Things that cause a sense of disgust

__________ = 2. OJRCALU
Characterized by joking

__________ = 3. MTONTU
The meat of sheep

__________ = 4. ATPSHMAN
Creation of the imagination or fancy; fantasy

__________ = 5. IRPOUOSIGD
Extraordinary in size, amount, extent, degree, force, etc.

__________ = 6. ITDECONRE
Dealing with very profound or difficult subject matter

__________ = 7. LASOH
Sandbank or sand bar in a body of water exposed at low tide

__________ = 8. CEUDTNATR
Shortened by or as if by having a part cut off; cut short

__________ = 9. LERTIITNAACU
Lacking the ability to express oneself, esp. in clear speech

__________ = 10. DUAYG
Brilliantly or excessively showy

__________ = 11. MSHRSAICOANN
Persons, objects, or practices that belong to a different time period

__________ = 12. SEENTCDAO
Short accounts of interesting or humorous incidents

__________ = 13. UETEATNDTA
To make thin; to make slender or fine

__________ = 14. ALMCAITY
Great misfortune or disaster

__________ = 15. SLOASLCO
Extraordinarily great in size, extent, or degree; gigantic; huge

__________ = 16. ETADEDCN
In a condition or process of mental or moral decay

__________ = 17. GYDEIND
Swirling as if in a whirlpool

__________ = 18. OVUFSROUGIR
Feeding on fruit; fruit eating

__________ = 19. ERVSIGIRD
A blue-green crust formed on copper, brass, or bronze surfaces
exposed to the atmosphere for long periods of time

ABOMINATIONS	= 1.	NNIMATIAOOBS Things that cause a sense of disgust
JOCULAR	= 2.	OJRCALU Characterized by joking
MUTTON	= 3.	MTONTU The meat of sheep
PHANTASM	= 4.	ATPSHMAN Creation of the imagination or fancy; fantasy
PRODIGIOUS	= 5.	IRPOUOSIGD Extraordinary in size, amount, extent, degree, force, etc.
RECONDITE	= 6.	ITDECONRE Dealing with very profound or difficult subject matter
SHOAL	= 7.	LASOH Sandbank or sand bar in a body of water exposed at low tide
TRUNCATED	= 8.	CEUDTNATR Shortened by or as if by having a part cut off; cut short
INARTICULATE	= 9.	LERTIITNAACU Lacking the ability to express oneself, esp. in clear speech
GAUDY	= 10.	DUAYG Brilliantly or excessively showy
ANACHRONISMS	= 11.	MSHRSAICOANN Persons, objects, or practices that belong to a different time period
ANECDOTES	= 12.	SEENTCDAO Short accounts of interesting or humorous incidents
ATTENUATED	= 13.	UETEATNDTA To make thin; to make slender or fine
CALAMITY	= 14.	ALMCAITY Great misfortune or disaster
COLOSSAL	= 15.	SLOASLCO Extraordinarily great in size, extent, or degree; gigantic; huge
DECADENT	= 16.	ETADEDCN In a condition or process of mental or moral decay
EDDYING	= 17.	GYDEIND Swirling as if in a whirlpool
FRUGIVOROUS	= 18.	OVUFSROUGIR Feeding on fruit; fruit eating
VERDIGRIS	= 19.	ERVSIGIRD A blue-green crust formed on copper, brass, or bronze surfaces exposed to the atmosphere for long periods of time

www.ingramcontent.com/pod-product-compliance
Lightning Source LLC
Chambersburg PA
CBHW080256030726
47593CB00009B/2512